CHAMPIONSHIP
FOOTBALL

by 12 Great Coaches

Compiled and Edited by

Tom Ecker and Paul Jones

Englewood Cliffs, N. J.

PRENTICE-HALL, INC.

Third printing......January, 1964

PRINTED IN THE UNITED STATES OF AMERICA
12740—BC

Preface

The first intercollegiate football game was played in 1869 between Princeton and Rutgers, but there was little resemblance between that 6 to 4 Rutgers victory and the football games we know today: The ball was round. No passing or running was permitted. There were 25 players on each team.

Although modern-day football barely resembles the rough and tumble game that was the rage of college campuses almost a century ago, the changes have actually come about gradually. Teams were cut to eleven men in 1880; tackling below the waist was legalized in 1888; the forward pass was introduced in 1906 and popularized in 1913; the use of the huddle was developed in the early 1920's.

Of course, the game of football could never have evolved to its present high level without the great coaches of the past who devoted their lives to the betterment of the game. Men like Walter Camp, Amos Alonzo Stagg, Fielding H. Yost, Glenn S. "Pop" Warner, and Knute Rockne laid the foundation for the game that is played today. Their contributions will never be forgotten.

Today, carrying on in the tradition of the outstanding coaches of the past, are their modern-day counterparts— great coaches who, with their ingenuity and wizardry, continue to revolutionize the ever-changing game of football. In this one volume, *Championship Football,* twelve of the most brilliant and successful of these twentieth century coaches have collaborated to bring their time-tested coach-

v

ing methods to the coaches, athletes, and fans of this country. These twelve men have won 1027 games during their 180 total years as head coaches and have been honored again and again for their many contributions to football.

Most of the material for this book was collected through a series of tape-recorded interviews with the coaches. The first interview was held in the Nittany Mountains of Pennsylvania. The final interview was held five months and 7300 miles later in a downtown Chicago hotel.

We are proud to have had the opportunity to work with these twelve great coaches and to have had a part in one of their many contributions to the game of football.

ACKNOWLEDGMENTS

For their help in putting together this book, our sincere thanks to Larry Perry, Russell Banks, Jack Griffin, Mike Campbell, Hayden Fry, Gene Stallings, Dr. Eugene Stish, and Bob Harville.

And again we are deeply grateful to those who helped in the preparation of the manuscript, Judy Ecker and Richard Bell.

TOM ECKER
PAUL JONES

Contents

vii

CHAPTER ONE

Team Organization
and Morale

CHARLES A. "RIP" ENGLE
Penn State University

RIP ENGLE has never had a losing season at Penn State. His 12-year record shows 77 wins, 34 defeats, and four ties, including Liberty Bowl victories over Alabama in 1959 and Oregon in 1960, and a Gator Bowl win over Georgia Tech in 1961.

Engle began his coaching career at Waynesboro (Pa.) High School, where he logged an 11-year, 86-17-5 record, including three perfect seasons and eight conference titles. His teams lost only ten games during their last seven seasons.

After a year of graduate work at his alma mater, Engle moved to Brown University as an assistant coach in 1942, and up to the head job in 1944. In his six years at Brown, Engle brought the Bruins to a peak, winning 15 of 18 games his last two years there. These were the two best seasons in Brown's football history.

Besides his coaching duties at Penn State, Engle has served as president of the American Football Coaches Association, has journeyed twice to Europe and once to Japan to conduct coaching clinics for the Air Force, and has coached in five Blue-Gray games, three East-West Shrine games, and has twice coached the National All-Stars.

Team Organization and Morale

A football coach must also be a salesman. Although his more obvious tasks take place on the practice and playing fields, the coach has to be able to sell his program to the students and to the public if he expects it to be a success.

Through his relationship with the fans, the press, and the student body, the coach must try to interest as many people in football as he can. He can do a great deal by selling the students and townspeople on the fact that football is important to boys and that without everyone's complete support the program will suffer.

The coach must also see to it that the male members of the student body are interested in *playing* football. No coach has ever won football games without players. Some have lost games with them, but no one has ever won without them. Therefore, the coach must be able to sell the boys and their parents on the values of the football program.

The Values of Football

Many values can be derived from playing football—values that are going to help make the young athlete a better person and thus a better citizen.

First, football teaches the value of work. The football player not only learns how to be a part of a team, but he also learns how to work on his own. Each individual is soon aware that he improves in direct proportion to the amount of work that he does, no matter how much natural ability he has.

3

The football player also learns the importance of sound preparation. A football team must prepare for the coming season in a very short time and must make weekly game preparations during that season. Knowing the value of sound preparations can be carried over and put to good use in later life.

And of course, the football player learns the value of giving—the giving of himself and the giving of his time. He soon begins to realize the many sacrifices one must make in order to do well.

If football does not have these values, if the only importance is in the winning of games and in the amount of money that is put into the program or gotten out of it, then football cannot be defended as a worthwhile part of an educational institution. More must come out of football than just a winning season or making a few dollars.

Relationship Between Coach and Athlete

The type of relationship a coach will have with his boys depends largely upon the coach and his personality. Some coaches prefer to remain on a "high pedestal," keeping well away from their athletes. Others want to be close to their boys. Personally, I have always tried to maintain a friendly atmosphere, both on the field and off, where each boy knows that he has a friend—someone he can talk with when he has a problem.

Through the years I've heard many young men say that the greatest single influence on their lives has been their high school coach. Because a coach often has as much influence on a young boy as any teacher or minister, or sometimes even his parents, it is very important that the coach set a good example. He must be a good-hearted person, a fellow who believes in the Golden Rule and in the things that a parent wants his son to believe in.

To me the most enjoyable part of coaching is working with the boys. A coach may be a bit apprehensive as he faces the coming season or a particular game, but there is a feeling of confidence that always seems to come from the fellowship created by his team.

Obligations of the Athlete

Besides his actual performance on the practice field and in games, each football player has certain obligations to his school, to his coach, and to himself.

Since each boy's purpose in school is to get an education, that must always be his first consideration. If, after four years, a boy has developed his athletic ability fully but hasn't received a full education, he has definitely "short-changed" himself. Athletics should never be put ahead of a boy's education.

Each athlete also has obligations concerning his physical condition. We ask our boys to do the things that will keep them in the best condition and to refrain from doing anything that might deter from it. Our boys know that anyone who does not train properly will be dropped from the squad.

Preparing the Team

Our practice sessions begin three and a half weeks before the first game, giving us enough time to get the team ready, but not so much time that the practices become a drudgery.

All of our "rough work" is done during the first two weeks. This is the time when we find out who the members of our football team will be. If there is ever a time when the boys might become discouraged, it will be during these early practice sessions.

We usually practice for an hour and 45 minutes. Some of our early sessions do last longer, but even during those first two weeks we never practice for more than two hours at a time. It is generally agreed that after a two-hour workout, an athlete's efficiency drops appreciably and therefore the amount that can be accomplished diminishes.

After the first two weeks, we never scrimmage in practice except for an occasional pass scrimmage. More is accomplished by having the players work on coordination and agility drills, individual drills, and combination drills. Not only have we suffered fewer injuries, but the squad as a whole looks forward to the games with more enthusiasm when there is no scrimmage in practice.

Sometimes practice does get to be a drudgery. It isn't always fun to go out and "butt heads" day after day, so it is best to keep a little fun in the game whenever possible. Even if a few minutes of practice time are lost occasionally, it pays to keep the squad loose and enjoying the game.

If there is a boy on the squad who has a good sense of humor and the ability to make the squad laugh once in a while, he should not be discouraged. A great deal of football depends on team morale, so it is important to keep some fun in the game.

Rosie Greer was one who had a great sense of humor. If Milt Plum would call a play to Greer's side of the line in practice, Rosie would come bouncing out of the huddle saying, "Lovely! Lovely!" But one day after Plum had called several plays to the opposite side, Greer was becoming a bit downhearted. He looked at Plum and said, "Milton, remember what Coach says. 'Utilize your strengths!' "

Spring Practice

Spring practice helps us accomplish three things:
1. To find out what position each boy plays best.
2. To find out who our 30 best football players are.
3. To teach some fundamentals.

At the end of the spring practice sessions, our staff evaluates each boy—his strengths, weaknesses, and the factors that may help him to become a better football player. Then I personally interview each boy. This is a fine opportunity for the coach to get a little closer to each boy, helping to create the kind of relationship a coach must have with his team if he is to be successful.

Scheduling

The first thing a coach must remember when he is planning his schedule for coming seasons is: *You must play teams of importance in order to gain importance.* A team that defeats a far inferior team has accomplished nothing, for this is no challenge to a coach or to his team. On the other hand, it is no disgrace to lose to a very good football team.

Penn State's "Equal-Time" System

At Penn State two first teams are prepared—a starting team and an alternate unit which we call the "Reddy" team. We have found that a well-prepared, experienced, and rested alternate team, even though its personnel may not have as much ability, will play better than a tired starting team.

A coach who prepares only one team (or prepares two

but uses only one and a few substitutes), may prepare the substitutes as well as his first team, but he cannot give them as much experience. We have found that an experienced alternate unit, when fresh, will invariably outplay the starting team.

Also, there is a feeling of competition that is generated between the two teams when the "equal-time" system is used. The boys take great pride in their teams, and even if given the opportunity, would rather not switch from one team to the other. Dick Hoak, for example, had a chance his senior year to move from his quarterback position on the "Reddy" team to the starting unit, but he asked to stay with his own group. Such *esprit de corps* creates a high level of morale and a spirit of competition that is worthwhile for the entire team.

Usually the clock tells us when to switch teams in the game. After seven minutes, the starting team comes out and the "Reddy" team goes in. However, if the team that is in the game is in the process of making a drive, the teams are not switched. It would be a mistake morale-wise to take a team out when they are moving the ball well.

The equal-time system can also protect the team against a complete letdown during the game. If one team isn't doing well, the other team can be sent in to pick up the pace, providing a more consistent team performance throughout the game.

Morale

Squad morale, the "all for one and one for all" attitude that we want our athletes to have, is of tremendous importance to the coach and his team. The big games cannot be won without it. Pep rallies, when conducted in a sensible way, general spirit throughout the school, and student cheering can help create the right atmosphere for the team.

We never try to "fire up" the team for a particular game. If the game is an important one, we feel that the team members will come up on their own. Firing up the team with a pep talk may have some value, but using this as the sole method of building spirit will soon get old.

There are often games in which the coach must do something to keep his squad from getting overexcited. When his team is too tense, the coach must exert a quieting influence and try to relax them.

One of the biggest and perhaps most perplexing banes of a coach is overconfidence on the part of his team. It can happen to the most level-headed boys—and it often happens before the coach realizes. A difficult but necessary job for the coach is convincing his boys that the player who has his head in the clouds and his feet on the ground will soon find that they are both on the ground!

The Week of the Game

On Sunday our coaching staff goes over the scouting report of the team we are to face the following weekend, making our offensive and defensive plans for the game.

The report is presented to the squad at a meeting Monday evening. Each player is given a seven- or eight-page scout report which includes a rundown on each individual that they will be playing against, the strengths and weaknesses of the team, and our own plan of attack. In addition to this report, the quarterbacks are given a simple game plan.

Lenny Moore, Penn State halfback now with the Baltimore Colts.

Richie Lucas, all-American quarterback at Penn State.

When discussing opponents at these meetings, we try to be completely honest with our boys. We have often said, "This team isn't as good as the team we played last week, but they can beat us if we let down." Or we have said, "This team is better than we are, so we're going to have to work hard in order to beat them."

Of course the coach should never present a game as a hopeless situation, no matter how formidable the opposition is. A team that goes into a game believing that it is impossible to win will find that it *IS* impossible to win.

The week's practice schedule is as follows:

MONDAY—Light practice followed by a squad meeting in which the scout reports are given out. A film of the previous week's game is usually shown in part.

TUESDAY AND *WEDNESDAY*—Heavy practice with demonstrations by members of the coaching staff and repeated application by members of the squad.

THURSDAY—Lighter practice to taper off the week's work.

FRIDAY—20-minute practice in sweat clothes, reviewing some of the problems that might be encountered in the next day's game, followed by a squad meeting in which key situations are diagrammed on the blackboard. Often a film of the opposition is shown.

On the day of the game, the squad takes the field for the pre-game warmup of loosening exercises, kicking and passing, starts, and group drills. After 14 minutes on the field, the team returns to the locker room for any last-minute instructions. The team captain then says a few words to the squad and they are ready to go out on the field for the game.

In the game, we believe the team should be run from the field—not from the bench. The quarterback calls the offensive plays; one linebacker (usually our center) calls defensive line signals; the quarterback decides what defensive set-up will be used in the secondary; the team captain makes all other decisions. When the quarterback or the defensive signal callers are out of the game, we give them added instructions.

At halftime we correct the mistakes that were made in the first half and offer any ideas that might improve the team's second-half performance.

Immediately after the game, we all get together in the dressing room to bow our heads and silently count our blessings, giving each individual an opportunity to make a few promises to himself and to come out a much better boy. Win or lose, there is a fine feeling that goes with this post-game prayer.

Then the boys get dressed and are on their way.

CHAPTER TWO

Conditioning
Football Players

Murray Warmath
University of Minnesota

MURRAY WARMATH, head football coach at the University of Minnesota since 1954, is known in the coaching field as a man of conviction. Although he suffered through a number of rather bleak seasons during his early years at Minnesota, Warmath stood firmly on his football beliefs and brought the Gophers from the bottom of the Big Ten to the top in 1960, winning the national championship and earning a place in the Rose Bowl.

Warmath's 1961 team was almost as good, posting an 8-2 season record and adding an impressive 21-3 win over UCLA in the 1962 Rose Bowl. For his coaching accomplishments, Warmath was named coach of the year by the American Football Coaches Association, the Football Writers Association, the Columbus (Ohio) Touchdown Club, the Los Angeles Times, the Dapper Dan Club of Pittsburgh, the Knute Rockne Club, and *Coach & Athlete* magazine.

During his undergraduate days, Warmath played guard under General Bob Neyland at the University of Tennessee and, after graduation, he served as assistant coach there. Before joining the Minnesota staff, Warmath also coached at Mississippi State and the U. S. Military Academy at West Point.

Conditioning Football Players

Football players must be well-conditioned—both physically and mentally—if they are expected to do their best. When all other things are equal, the team that is in the best condition usually wins.

Good physical condition is important to the football player for a number of reasons: First, it helps protect him against injuries which might eliminate him from competition. Second, it gives him greater strength, which will make him more proficient in performing his football skills. And third, it gives him more stamina and endurance, enabling him to perform well for a longer period of time.

Mental conditioning may be even more important to the athlete than his physical condition. Mental conditioning is mental discipline and morale. More specifically, it is the willingness of the athlete to "pay the price" and do everything that is necessary to prepare himself for a game. Mental conditioning should never be overlooked by the coach since it often determines the attitude of his entire team.

When going through a conditioning program, boys often suffer physical and mental pain. If a boy is not in good physical condition and he reaches the point of fatigue, his morale begins to decline and his mental condition lags. Hard work and continued talk about the "will to win" is the only way to arrive at good physical condition and a winning attitude. This is an area where the coach gives his personality to his team, and they in return begin to reflect the attitude of the coach.

Fall Conditioning

Our conditioning program begins with the fall practice sessions. These sessions are planned so that they end with drills that involve a great deal of running—the best overall conditioner. Usually the running is done as part of drills that will prepare them for game situations, such as covering kick-offs or punts, but sometimes the players finish a mid-week practice session with wind sprints. When they run wind sprints, the players line up and run 40- or 50-yard sprints over and over until they are out of breath. Then they run a few more.

Our practice sessions last from an hour and forty-five minutes to two hours on Monday, Tuesday, and Wednesday. On Thursday we work for about an hour and on Friday about 15 minutes. Very little running is done on the Thursday and no running is done on the Friday before a game.

Spring Conditioning

In the spring, practice sessions run for at least two hours, but there is less concern about the athletes' physical condition than during the football season. Our primary interest in the spring is the teaching of good football techniques. However, since our spring practices are long and hard, the players automatically become well-conditioned physically.

Weight Training

To us, weight training is like an insurance policy. The muscle pad that athletes build on top of their shoulders, the additional muscle tone, and the strengthening of their joints and ligaments serve to protect them from injury.

All of our players take part in the weight training program during the winter and summer months, but not in the fall or spring when we are practicing football. When these athletes are working hard in practice every day, they do not need any additional work.

In the weight program at Minnesota, lifting is done only every other day, with the emphasis on strengthening the shoulder muscles, the abdominal muscles, the neck, and the knee joints against possible injuries. Then on the days that the boys are not in the weight room, they go through running and agility exercises.

It is very important that the athletes know how to exercise with weights properly. Since improper lifting may cause serious injuries, each boy's weight training is supervised during his first year to make sure that he learns the proper lifting techniques. Then, after his first year, the athlete is given a schedule that he is expected to follow during the summer and winter months.

The weight training program that we follow was devised by Dr. Eugene E. Stish of the University of Minnesota. This program outlines a systematic method of developing increased strength and muscular endurance in athletes through weight training.

WEIGHT TRAINING PROGRAM*

General Rules

1. All exercises must be performed to the maximum number of repetitions possible.

---

* Dr. Eugene E. Stish, "Weight Training Program" (University of Minnesota Department of Physical Education and Athletics, 1962).

NAME _____ SPORT _____

Exercise	Date Rep.	Wt.	Date Rep.	Wt.	Date Rep.	Wt.	Date Rep.	Wt.	Date Rep.	Wt.	Date Rep.	Wt.	Date Rep.	Wt.
1.														
2.														
3.														
4.														
5.														
6.														
7.														
8.														
9.														
10.														
11.														
12.														
13.														

FIG. 1

2. If the number of repetitions possible greatly exceeds 10 (e.g. 16 or more) then the weight should be increased for that exercise at the next workout.

3. If the number of repetitions possible is much less than 10 (e.g. 6 or less) than the weight should be decreased for that exercise at the next workout.

4. Do not exercise two days in succession—a Monday, Wednesday, Friday Program is most desirable in the initial phase.

5. Follow the same sequence of exercises each time you work out so that you will always be at the same relative stage of fatigue each time you perform a particular exercise.

6. Keep a careful record of each workout. (See Figure 1.) Indicate weight used and number of repetitions performed for each exercise. Be certain to indicate the date on your card for each workout. If you do not perform certain exercises on a particular day, just draw a short dash through the appropriate square for that exercise.

7. A wise safety precaution for beginners is to prohibit performing exercises with weights which the performer cannot lift into position, i.e., which require aid from others to raise into starting position.

8. The weight training program should be under constant close supervision by a competent person.

9. Take necessary action to ensure protection of the floor at all times.

Specific Exercises

Pull-ups—Start from the straight-arm hanging position on the horizontal bar. The hand grip may be either the forward, reverse, or alternate. Pull the body upward until the chin is over the bar and then lower the body until the arms are straight again. Continue these movements steadily as many times as possible. When you are finally unable to complete the full upward movement, then make 8-10 all-out attempts to do so before releasing the bar. Do not use a kicking, jerking, or a "kip" action. Record the number of successful pull-ups and your body weight for that day.

Sit-ups—Start from a relaxed position on your back on the sit-up board with the feet and ankles hooked under the ankle-rope. The hands should be clasped behind the head and the knees may be slightly bent. Raise yourself to the sitting position and then slowly back to the starting position. Touch alternate elbows to the opposite knee as you come up to the sitting position. The difficulty of the exercise may be increased, and thus the number of repetitions decreased, by placing the foot-end of the sit-up board higher up on the stall-bars. Sit-ups may also be performed while holding a weight (dumbell or barbell) behind the neck.

Record the number of sit-ups performed and the height of the sit-up board and/or the weights used.

Walking-Squats—Place the barbell behind the head and resting on the shoulders and hold it with both hands. Begin with feet together, head and shoulders erect and back straight. Take a short step (heel of front foot 3-4 inches ahead of toe of rear foot and feet 2-4 inches apart laterally) with either foot and go into a squat position until the thigh of the forward leg is approximately horizontal. Return to the erect position, step forward with the other foot and repeat the squat movement. Keep the back and upper body as erect and near vertical as possible. Squatting so deeply that the thigh of the forward leg goes beyond the horizontal can result in injury to the knee joint. Record the total number of squats done by either leg and the weight used.

Heel Raise—Begin with the barbell across the shoulders, holding it with both hands. Stand with both feet on the edge of a plank or platform at least 2 inches high with the body weight supported on the toes and the ball of the foot. Keep the body erect and the head up at all times. Raise the whole body upward as far as possible by extending the feet at the ankles. Then, by flexing the feet, slowly lower the body, maintaining erect posture, as far down as possible without touching the heels to the floor. Repeat this movement as many times as possible. Do not rest the heels on the floor. Keep the movement slow, continuous, and controlled at all times. Record the number of times the movement cycle is completed and the weight used.

Pull Over—Begin in the supine position (lying down on the back) with arms extended on the floor beyond the head. Grasp the weight (barbell or dumbells) with a forward grasp. Keeping the arms and body straight, raise and move

Tom Brown, weight-trained all-American guard at Minnesota.

Greg Larson, Minnesota center now with the New York Giants, concentrated on weight training throughout college.

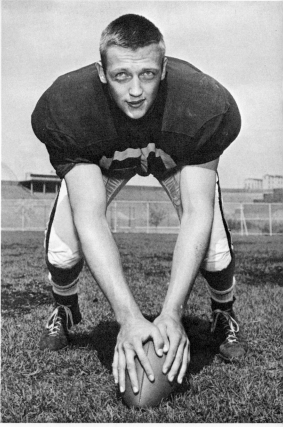

the weight, by action at the shoulder, until the weight is being held just above the abdomen. Then reverse the movement and return the weight to its starting position. After the exercise has started do not rest the weight on the floor or on the body. Keep the arms and body straight at all times. The exercise should be continuous and controlled throughout. Record the number of times the exercise cycle is completed and the weight used.

Lateral Raise Supine—Begin in the supine position with arms extended straight out laterally from the shoulders. Grasp the dumbells in each hand with the palms up. Raise the weights upward to a position vertically above the body. Do not bend the elbows or change the movement from a perpendicular plane. Lower the weights back to the starting position but do not rest them on the floor. Keep the movement cycle going steadily as long as possible. Control all movements of the weight. Do not let gravity increase velocity on the downward movement. Record number of times the exercise cycle is completed and the weight used.

Lateral Raise Prone—Begin in the prone (face down) position on the exercise table with the arms hanging vertically downward. The head and shoulders must be extended over the end of the table sufficiently to allow full lateral movement of the shoulders. Hold the dumbells in your hands (palms inward) and raise the weights upward laterally in a plane perpendicular to the length of your body. Continue the lateral movement as far as possible, raising the head and arching the back at the same time. Return the weights again to the starting position and continue the cycle. Keep the movement controlled at all times. Do not "throw" the weights on the upward movement or let them "fall" on the downward movement. Record the number of times the exercise cycle is completed and the weight used.

Lateral Raise Standing—Begin in an erect position standing as tall as possible. Hold arms at sides with dumbells in hands and with palms facing inward. Raise the weights laterally and upward (in the same plane) as far as possible and then return the weights to the starting position. Do not rotate the forearm (i.e. turn the palm upward) or bend the elbow during the exercise. Maintain constant control over all movements so that the exercise is performed at a steady rate. Record the number of times the exercise cycle is completed and the weight used.

Forward Raise—Begin in an erect position standing as tall as possible. Hold arms at sides with dumbells in hands and with palms facing inward. Raise the weights forward and upward (in parallel planes) as far as possible and then return the weights to the starting position. Do not rotate the forearm or bend the elbow during the exercise. Maintain constant control over all movements so that the exercise is performed at a steady rate. Record the number of times the exercise cycle is completed and the weight used.

Press—Hold the barbell in front of the chest with the palms of the hands facing away from the body. Stand as tall and erect as possible and raise the weight upward until the arms are fully extended above the head. Return to the starting position and then repeat the cycle. Be sure to keep the body erect at all times so that the press is parallel to the long axis of the body. Undesirable arching of the back may be prevented by performing the press with the back next to a wall. Record the number of times the exercise cycle is completed and the weight used.

Arm Curls—Hold the dumbells or barbell down at the thigh with the arms fully extended and palms facing forward. Begin the movement with flexion of the wrists and then continue raising the weight forward and upward with flexion at the elbow. Continue the upward movement until the elbow is flexed as far as possible and then return to the starting position. Maintain the elbows and upper arms fixed in relation to the body and do not arch the back. Perform the exercise at a steady rate in both upward and downward movements. Record the number of times the exercise cycle is completed and the weight used.

Wrist Curls—Begin with palms up and forearms resting on the table, and with the wrists, hands, and dumbells hanging over the edge of the table. Allow the weight to roll down on the finger tips as far as possible and then begin the curling movement with the fingers, then the hand, and finally the wrist, curling it upward as far as possible. Follow the reverse procedure in returning to the starting position. Be certain that the floor is protected beneath your weights in case you drop them. Record the number of times the exercise cycle is completed and the weight used.

Wrist Extensions—Begin with palms down and forearms resting on the table, and with the wrists, hands, and dumbells hanging over the edge of the table. Allow the weight to roll down on the finger tips as far as possible and then begin to curl the fingers and then the hand. Then bring the wrist upward in extensions as far as possible. Follow the reverse procedure in returning to the starting position. Record the number of times the exercise cycle is completed and the weight used.

Trunk Twister—Stand erect in a well-balanced position with feet apart. Hold the barbell with both hands (palms up) at about lower chest height. Turn to the right as far as possible without moving the feet and then swing fairly rapidly as far to the left as possible. Then return to the right in the same manner. *CAUTION:* This exercise can be dangerous if not performed in a *steady* and *controlled* manner. Do not let the weight pull you at any time—*you* move the weight. Record the number of times the exercise is performed to each side and the weight used.

Weight Training Equipment

It will save time and afford better control over the progressive increase of the resistance in exercises if the dumbells and barbells to be used are permanently set up and clearly marked as to their weight. Then the participant will not expend time and energy taking apart and putting together the various weights and will use the same weight each time rather than one "approximately" the same.

Commercially manufactured weights are easy to use and present a nice appearance, but it is not necessary to use them if to do so would put an impossible strain on the departmental budget. A little ingenuity practiced in the school shop with some pipe, tin cans, concrete, melted lead, old engine cylinders, etc. can result in a perfectly satisfactory set of weights. However, it is best to have at least one adjustable barbell of the commercial type which can be adjusted up to 225 pounds.

Plans for equipment should also include some type of storage shelves or racks for the weights and a clean, roomy, well-ventilated area in which to exercise. Precautions must also be taken to protect floors from damage by weights which might be dropped. Floor protection precautions may include provisions of mats or wooden pads on which to work and certainly must include education of the participants.

Following is a list of equipment for a program which would have approximately 8-10 men working at one time:

Dumbells—	*Barbells*—(one each)
5 pounds—1 pair	40 pounds
10 pounds—2 pairs	50 pounds
15 pounds—3 pairs	70 pounds
20 pounds—2 pairs	90 pounds
25 pounds—1 pair	110 pounds
	130 pounds
	150 pounds

Included in this list should be one barbell adjustable up to 225 pounds or fixed barbells at 10 or 20 pound intervals up to 200 pounds.

SUMMARY

The success of a football team is often dependent upon how well the team is conditioned—both physically and mentally. Players that are not well-conditioned cannot perform at their best.

Good physical and mental condition can only be attained through hard work and a proper attitude on the part of the coach and his team. They must work hard to develop the strength, stamina, and morale that is so necessary for success in football.

CHAPTER THREE

Offensive Line Play

JIM OWENS
University of Washington

JIM OWENS was named head football coach at the University of Washington in 1957, and since then has established himself as one of the outstanding coaches in the country. His 1959 and 1960 teams were the top ranked elevens on the Pacific Coast and the 1960 team was rated number one in the nation by the Helms Athletic Foundation. Both squads held 9-1 records and both were triumphant over the best of the Big Ten in the Rose Bowl.

Owens came to Washington with a solid football background. He played his collegiate football for the late Jim Tatum and for Bud Wilkinson at the University of Oklahoma, where he won all-American honors, and then went on to play in his second Sugar Bowl game and in the Senior Bowl. After playing one year of professional ball with the Baltimore Colts, Owens served as assistant coach for six years under Paul "Bear" Bryant at Kentucky and Texas A & M.

Voted West Coast coach of the year in 1959 and 1960 and runner-up for national coach of the year in 1960, Owens has posted a fine 31-19-2 record at Washington.

Offensive Line Play

One of the greatest challenges that faces a football coach is coaching the offensive line. Because linemen seldom get as much public recognition as they deserve, it often takes a real selling job on the part of the coach to convince them of their importance to the team. As soon as linemen realize that the offense cannot go unless they themselves make it go, the linemen will feel that they are an integral part of the football team.

Proper Stance

There are two different stances for linemen, depending upon the type of offense that is being run:

1. A quick-hitting, straight-ahead type of offense requires a three- or four-point stance with weight evenly distributed between the linemen's hands and the balls of their feet.

2. An offense that emphasizes pulling linemen and two-on-one blocking demands a stance with less weight forward in order to facilitate the lineman's quick lateral movements.

In a well-balanced stance, the lineman's feet are as far apart as his shoulders and pointed straight upfield. His back is parallel with the ground with his head back far enough to comfortably see his opponent, but not braced back in an unrelaxed position. One or both of his hands are on the ground with fingers extended.

At the University of Washington, our linemen stagger their feet in a heel-to-toe arrangement. On the right side of the line, the right foot is back and the right hand is down on the ground. On the left side, the left foot is back and the left hand down.

The coach should spend a great deal of time watching his linemen to make sure they are not unconsciously tipping off the direction of plays. Good defensive linemen and linebackers will watch for any kind of tip. A lineman might stagger his feet differently or perhaps lean back slightly, thus helping the defense to diagnose the play.

By having his linemen assume the proper stance over and over in practice until it becomes a habit, a coach can eliminate many of these line "tip-offs." Then, even late in a game when the linemen are tired and thinking about something else, they will always assume the same stance because of the many practice hours they have put in.

Line Blocking

Before a lineman can do an intelligent job of blocking a defensive man, he must know:
1. The type of play that is being run.
2. The point of attack.
3. The best blocking techniques to use.
4. The count, so that he can get the jump on the defensive man.

To execute an effective line block, the blocker must make contact immediately and then keep contact so the defensive man cannot release and go to the play. The blocker gets off on the count, charging at the defensive man with head up and eyes open, and makes contact with his head or shoulder. Since it is the defensive lineman's goal to neutralize the offensive charge and then release to pursue the ball carrier, the blocker must keep pressure on the defensive man. He does this by following through on his block with a hard-driving, continuing action until the defensive man has been eliminated from effective pursuit of the ball carrier or until the play is over.

Offensive linemen must be able to adjust quickly to various defensive changes. Many defensive linemen move from one defensive position to another just before the ball is snapped, calling for a quick adjustment on the part of the blocker. Also, it is not at all uncommon for defensive linemen to loop or slant after the ball is snapped, making the offensive lineman's job even more challenging.

The center has the most demanding job in the offensive line since he must not only master the same blocking techniques as the other linemen, but he must also snap the ball properly on every play. The center is a vital part of the team, not only for exchanging the ball, but also for his point of attack blocking on interior plays. An offense that does not have a good center is seriously handicapped.

One-on-one block. The purpose of the one-on-one block is to remove a defensive man from the point of attack, or at least to neutralize him so that the area is clear enough for the offensive play. When executing a one-on-one block, the blocker is on his own. The only help he might have would be from an effective fake in the backfield, or perhaps from the quick-hitting speed of the ball carrier.

Two-on-one block. The present trend seems to be toward running more and more plays that require two-on-one blocking. The two-on-one is difficult to coach, but it is very effective because it provides a two against one situation; thus the blockers should have no trouble removing the defensive man from the point of attack.

Kurt Gegner, all-American tackle at Washington.

Bill Kinnune, one of Coach Owens' great linemen at Washington.

One of the blockers stops the charge of the defensive man with a post block. Then, as soon as the defender's charge has been neutralized, the other blocker makes contact from the side. Working together, the two blockers can turn the defensive man down the line to widen the hole for the play, or take him straight back to help "wall off" some of the defensive pursuit.

Trap block. At Washington, all linemen must be able to pull and trap. In our offense, not only the guards and tackles, but even the ends—and occasionally even the backs—trap linemen.

The trap block is much easier to execute if the defensive man has come across the line of scrimmage. However, a good trapper can make the block, even if the defensive man has not committed himself, by angling across the line of scrimmage to meet him.

The trapper must be in a balanced position when he delivers the blow, and then he must keep driving after contact has been made. A block that does not have a good follow-through is not a good block.

Cut-off block. The cut-off block is used by all of our linemen upon occasion, but it is used most often by the center. It is used to impede the pursuit of a lineman or linebacker on wide running plays. The cut-off blocker makes no initial contact with the defensive man but springs from one side of him to the other, cutting off his angle of pursuit.

Pin block. The pin block is used on many of our play passes. The blocker makes contact with his shoulder and then immediately goes into a body block or "pin." The blocker is first concerned with stopping the charge and then with containing the defensive man to keep him away from the passer.

Downfield Blocking

Good downfield blocking requires even more second effort and desire than line blocking does. It is natural for a blocker to slow up and start back for the huddle when he feels the play is almost over. It is the coach's job to teach his blockers to keep following through with their blocks until the play is *definitely* over.

Rather than blocking according to specific assignments, our downfield blockers sprint to predetermined downfield areas. When a defensive man shows up in a blocker's area, he immediately commits himself to a side body block. He throws the block as high as possible, hitting the defender with his hip, and then, as they hit the ground, follows through with a continuous scramble.

If the blocker is leading the ball carrier down the field, a different type of downfield block is required. Instead of throwing a side body block, the blocker keeps his feet and forces the defensive man to play him off, giving the ball carrier a chance to break away.

Protecting the Passer

The lineman's primary responsibility on pass plays is to keep his body between the defensive man and the passer. At the same time, he must try to keep the defensive man as low as possible, so the charger cannot get his hands up to deflect the pass or to cause the passer to loft the ball too much.

On play passes, the blocking is very aggressive. The linemen fire out on the count to try to make the pass play look as much like a running play as possible.

Delayed passes, initially, require a more passive-type blocking. On the snap of the ball, the linemen drop back and form a cup to protect the area from which the pass will be thrown. Then, from that point, the blocking becomes *very* aggressive.

Protecting the Punter

From spread punt formation, the linemen block aggressively for a certain length of time, giving the punter time to recover in case of a bad snap or fumbled ball, and then release to cover their designated areas. If a coach is fortunate enough to have a center who can rifle the ball back 14 or 15 yards with accuracy, he can spread his men out across the field and cover immediately when the ball is snapped.

From tight punt formation, the blocking is extremely important, since the punter is not very deep in the backfield. The linemen protect the kicking area just as they protect the passing area on delayed pass plays. The blocks are held until the linemen hear the ball punted. Then they release and cover.

CHAPTER FOUR

Offensive Backfield Play

Frank Broyles
University of Arkansas

FRANK BROYLES has had phenomenal success since becoming head coach at Arkansas in 1958. After losing the first six games of the '58 season, the Razorbacks bounced back to win the last four. Then followed a tie for the Southwest Conference championship in 1959, a clear-cut title in 1960, and another tie for first place in 1961, making Broyles only the second coach in SWC history to win or tie for three consecutive titles. During this period, the Porkers won 28 of 34 regular season games.

Few men have ever had better training as an assistant coach than Broyles. He served for three years under Bob Woodruff at Baylor, where he helped develop some of the top quarterbacks in the Southwest Conference. Then Broyles returned to Georgia Tech, where he had starred at quarterback during the midforties, to begin a six-year tenure under the great Bobby Dodd.

Broyles was a versatile athlete when he was a student at Georgia Tech, winning ten varsity letters and twice making the all-Southeastern Conference football and basketball teams. In the 1945 Orange Bowl (one of the four major bowl games in which he played), Broyles set a bowl passing record that still stands (17 completions for 286 yards).

Offensive Backfield Play

The ideal offensive attack consists of an even balance between the running game and the passing game.

The running game should combine speed, power, and deception. By being able to hit any spot along the line of scrimmage with maximum speed or power, and by being deceptive with fakes close to the line of scrimmage, the offense should move the ball consistently.

Of course, the success of the passing game depends upon the abilities of the passer and his receivers. If a good passer is available, it is wise to spend a great deal of time working on the passing game. Practices should be held on a lined-off field, alternating the position of the ball between the left hash mark, the middle of the field, and the right hash mark, so that every game situation will present itself. If a good passer is not available, then a good runner should be placed in the quarterback position.

Position and Stance of Backs

Quarterback position and stance. The quarterback stands behind the center, his feet parallel to each other and spread shoulder-width apart. Keeping his back straight, the quarterback assumes his position by bending his knees as though he were sitting down. His weight is distributed evenly on the balls of both feet so he can move with ease in any direction.

The quarterback's right hand is placed under the center's "tail," slightly to the right of center, with palm down and fingers spread apart. He next places his left hand below the right, slightly to the left of center, with his left thumb under the thumb of his right hand. He is then in position to receive the ball.

Fullback position and stance. The fullback takes a position four yards behind the center. His is a three-point stance with feet parallel to each other and spread shoulder-width apart. One hand touches the ground with fingers extended, but little weight is placed on it. The fullback's weight is distributed evenly between his feet so that he can start quickly to either side or straight ahead.

Halfback position and stance. In the T formation, each halfback lines up in a position relative to the fullback. To determine the position of the two halfbacks, the fullback takes his position in the backfield and extends his arms to the sides. The halfbacks then line up on either side of him with their arms extended, moving toward or away from the fullback until their fingertips barely touch. They are then the correct distance apart.

The halfbacks should be about a foot nearer the line of scrimmage than the fullback. This distance is determined by having the halfback place the heel of his outside foot in line with the fullback's toes.

The halfback takes a three-point stance with his inside hand on the ground, supporting a considerable amount of his weight. The inside foot is placed a few inches back to help insure quick movement to the inside, as well as straight ahead.

Wingback position and stance. When running from the Winged T formation, the wingback lines up one yard outside the end and one yard off the line of scrimmage. He faces in at an angle of 45 degrees.

His is a two-point stance, feet spread shoulder-width apart, with hands on his knees.

Slotback position and stance. When running from the Slotback formation, the end is split out and the slotback lines up one yard outside and one yard behind the tackle. The slotback's stance is the same as the wingback's.

Exchanging the Ball

The back who is to receive the ball sprints to the point of exchange, keeping his head and eyes up and focusing his attention on the defense. He never looks at the quarterback or the ball.

When receiving the ball from the quarterback, the back must always create a pocket in which to receive the ball. He does this by placing his outside arm across his body about belt high and his inside arm across his chest. (See Figure 2.)

FIG. 2

To help prevent fumbles, the back cups his hands over the ends of the ball as soon as it is placed in the pocket. He then puts the ball away, with both hands still holding it, by "riding it back" under his arm. Both hands remain on the ball until he is "across the street"—a point five yards past the line of scrimmage.

Faking

At Arkansas two different kinds of fakes are used. In one, the quarterback turns his back to the line of scrimmage and fakes an empty hand to the faking back while holding the ball close to his body with the other hand. As the faking back passes, the quarterback pulls his hand back out of the pocket as though he had made the handoff.

In our second type of fake, the quarterback faces the line of scrimmage so the defense can see the handling of the ball. As the faking back passes, the quarterback places the ball in the pocket and rides along with him, keeping both hands on the ball. Then at the last moment he pulls the ball back out of the pocket, completing the fake.

Running With the Ball

After the ball-carrier "crosses the street," he takes one hand off the ball so he can use it to help ward off tacklers. To help insure against fumbling when carrying the football with only one hand, the ball-carrier's fingers are spread over one end of the ball while the other end rides in the cradle formed between the runner's upper arm and chest. Then, to keep from fumbling when he is about to be tackled, the ball-carrier again uses his free hand to help hold onto the ball.

Fly Technique

Using a flyman in the backfield is a technique that can add strength to a team's offensive attack. The flyman is a wingback who, just before the snap of the ball, is set in motion back to a point near where he would have been positioned in the normal backfield lineup.

If the defense overshifts toward the wingback, our team will be running a balanced offense against an overshifted defense. If the defense does not overshift, our team can run toward the wingback, giving added strength to his side. Either situation creates a weakness in their defense.

COACHING THE QUARTERBACK

The most important of all of the backfield positions, and the one that should be given first consideration by the coach when selecting his personnel, is the quarterback position. It is the key to a successful offense.

There is no question that the quarterback has the most demanding position on the team. Besides the obvious physical abilities he must have, the quarterback has to be a forceful leader. He must have poise and confidence on the field in order to gain the confidence and respect of his teammates.

The quarterback must also be intelligent. Since he is the "field general," he must recognize the strengths and weaknesses of each of the defenses he faces, and then be able to exploit his own team's strengths as well as his opponent's weaknesses.

Other traits that the outstanding quarterback must have are good personality and temperament, a lot of pep, and plenty of enthusiasm for the game of football.

Jim Mooty, all-American halfback at Arkansas.

Lance Alworth, all-American halfback at Arkansas.

Preparing the Quarterback

We believe that the proper selection of plays is the most important factor in winning games. Since it is apparent that the quarterback must be able to call the right play at the right time, he must be taught certain basic principles upon which his calls will be used.

Before the quarterback can be sure of making the best calls, he must first have a thorough knowledge of his overall offense and the capabilities of each of his teammates. Next he must be able to recognize and know how to cope with every conceivable type of defense. And finally, he must know the general rules for play selection. Then we go over our own offense with the quarterback and show him how he can attack a particular defense and defeat it.

Game Strategy

The strategy our quarterback employs during a particular game depends largely upon our pre-game plans. Prior to every game we will know something about the strengths, weaknesses, and types of defenses used by the opponent. From this information our general strategy plans are set up.

It is never wise to play blindly on the basis of these pre-game plans, however, since many things may occur during the course of a game to alter those plans. They are merely a start. Information gained as the game progresses determines the changes made in our game strategy.

The type of defense that the opponent uses and its characteristics will determine our offensive attack.

Against a stunting defense. The quarterback may find faking quick running plays and throwing short passes to be effective against a stunting defense. Also, option-type plays at an end who is stunting may be successful. Backs in motion, flankers, or split ends will often eliminate most of the stunting used by the defensive team.

Against a penetrating defense. When facing a penetrating defense, the quarterback will probably have the most success with quick pitch-outs, screen passes, traps, and the fake pass-and-run. Seldom is there time to throw the long pass.

Against a waiting defense. The waiting defense presents the quarterback with many problems. Power plays through the line or wide plays that follow a good inside fake may be successful. Since the waiting defense does not rush well, the quarterback usually has plenty of time to throw the long pass.

General Rules for the Quarterback

1. Know your own offense thoroughly.
2. Know the capabilities of each teammate.
3. Find out as much as you can about every opponent.
4. Know what defenses to expect.
5. Know how to penetrate the various defenses with your offense.
6. Know when to use flankers, wingbacks, and split ends.
7. Know what to call in critical situations.
8. Always call plays with force and confidence.
9. Permit no talking in the huddle.
10. If the opponent is short of reserve strength, play a hard-hitting, bruising game in an effort to wear the team down physically.
11. Every call should be made with a purpose in mind, based on the over-all strategy.

12. Special plays may be effective either early in the game against an opponent that has prepared well for the basic attack, or later in the game when the opponent begins limiting the success of the basic attack.

13. When any defensive weakness is spotted, direct the attack at it before it can be corrected.

14. Play faster when the wind is to your back; slower when you are facing the wind.

15. When using flankers, watch the defense. If they shift toward the flanker, run to the opposite side. If they do not shift, run toward the flanker.

16. Avoid running the same play in the same situation every time.

17. If the opposing team has a reckless, hard-charging line, concentrate on traps, counters, reverses, and screen passes.

18. The element of surprise is one of your most useful weapons. Use it wisely! Catching an opponent off guard can often compensate for a lack of offensive strength.

19. When your team is behind, open up your offense with special plays and passes in an effort to catch up. You have nothing to lose by taking chances when behind.

20. Do not have definite rules for when to pass.

21. Plays that involve a lot of ball-handling or sharp turns should be avoided when the field is wet.

22. When the field is wet or muddy, it is best to kick and let the opponent do the fumbling.

23. Be alert! If you see a defensive back limping during the game, throw a pass in his area. If you see a lineman limping, run a play over him.

24. When your team is backed up to the goal line, do not take chances with passes or slow developing plays, and do not wait until fourth down to kick.

25. Be careful when using special plays. Their failure could have an adverse effect on the team's morale.

26. When facing a strong head wind, it is not safe to throw anything other than short passes. When the wind is to your back, long passes may be very effective.

27. Do not always wait until a "passing down" to pass.

28. Know which defenders stop each play that you call and then make your calls with those facts in mind. Often when a particular defensive man makes the tackle on a play, the companion play or a check play may be successful.

29. When your team is behind with time running out, play fast and recklessly. When ahead, play a slow, conservative game.

30. Take advantage of the breaks. When one comes your way, score!

CHAPTER FIVE

The Passing Game

JACK CURTICE
Stanford University

JACK CURTICE has become known in football circles as Mr. Forward Pass. He has twice coached teams to national passing titles and is the only coach ever to win both the rushing and passing titles twice.

Curtice's 1957 Utah team produced the nation's leading passer, Lee Grosscup, and the nation's leading receiver, Stuart Vaughn, and still holds the NCAA major college record for the highest percentage of passes completed in a single season. (61.0%). Curtice's 1959 Stanford team, led by all-American end Chris Burford, still holds the NCAA record for the most passes completed in a single season (176). Burford, with 61 catches for 756 yards, led the nation in pass receiving that year while quarterback Dick Norman, completing 152 of 263 passes for 1,963 yards and 11 touchdowns, led the nation in passing and total offense.

As a college athlete, Curtice himself was an outstanding passer. During his junior year at Transylvania College, Curtice led the nation in passing, completing 23 touchdown aerials.

Long considered the authority on every phase of passing, Curtice is the author of a highly regarded book, *The Passing Game in Football.* (The Ronald Press, New York, N. Y., 1961.)

The Passing Game

A successful passing attack first requires good protection for the passer. Then, the receiver must be able to free himself from defenders and break into the clear at the right moment. And finally, with split-second timing, the passer must be able to put the ball in front of the receiver at the very moment the receiver breaks into the open. If the passer has good protection and throws the ball correctly, and if the receiver runs at top speed, there is no way to defend against a team's passing attack.

Opponents that respect the team's passing game have to keep depth in their secondary, giving the offense the opportunity to size up the defense and choose between running and passing. The defense will not be able to overload the line in order to stop just the running game.

The running game and the passing game actually compliment each other. A team must have a good passing attack in order to have a successful running attack, and, conversely, must have a good running attack in order to have a successful passing attack.

Developing the Passing Attack

It is often helpful in setting up a pass offense to look at it through the eyes of the defense. To try to stop the passing attack, the defensive team will probably do the following:

1. Rush the passer.
2. Hold up the receivers or force them out of their patterns.

3. Play the ball.
4. Rush heavily (eight men).
5. Drop off a large number (eight men).

If the pass offense is to be effective, these defensive efforts must be overcome by doing the following:

1. Insure adequate protection at all times, making it difficult to rush the passer.
2. Spread and isolate the receivers to make it difficult to hold them up, or knock them out of their patterns.
3. Take advantage of the type of defense in such a way that the passer will be able to deliver the pass quickly.
4. Make sure the ball is thrown at the proper time to eliminate the interception possibility.

Hard work is probably the most important factor in developing a successful passing attack. Our passers and receivers take such great pride in their work that they come out before practice every day to work on improving their passing and receiving techniques. The receivers go through their patterns, working on cuts and fakes, and the passers practice delivering the ball to the right spot at the exact moment the receiver is free.

Of course, the team that has a passer with a powerful arm and receivers with great innate ability has a definite advantage in developing its passing game. However, through hard work a team made up of boys with just ordinary ability can provide quite a passing threat through the use of sideline, hook, and jump passes.

The Passer

Ideally, the quarterback should be a threat as a runner as well as a passer. If the pass pattern breaks down, or if the passer is rushed heavily and cannot get the pass away, he has to be able to get out of the pocket and run the ball as best he can.

The passer must have poise, an even temperament, and the ability to think on his feet. And, he must be able to recognize and analyze each defensive formation.

Lee Grosscup, Coach Curtice' all-American quarterback at Utah. (Associated Press Wirephoto.)

The passer not only must be able to overcome the efforts of the defense to stop his passing attack, but he also must know the answers to questions concerning his own team:

1. Who is the best receiver on the team?
2. Which receiver runs the best patterns—especially on the hook, sideline, and sideline-and-up?
3. What pattern has the best percentage of completion?
4. How fast are the receivers? A passer must know this in order to lead the receivers correctly.
5. Who is the best runner? The screen pass should go to him.
6. Exactly when will the receiver make his cut? It is essential that the ball be delivered at the proper time.

The types of passes that we use are the drop back, roll out, running pass, jump pass, and screen pass. Having several different types of passes gives the team a variety of weapons to use in case the defense is changed to try to stop one particular type. It is very difficult for an opponent to be prepared for every type of pass.

There are eleven different principal spots from which these passes are thrown. (See Figure 3.) A pass from any

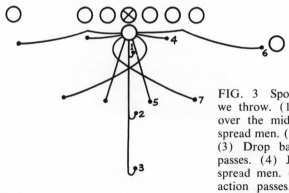

FIG. 3 Spots from which we throw. (1) Jump passes over the middle and to the spread men. (2) Short passes. (3) Drop back and screen passes. (4) Jump passes to spread men. (5) Short play-action passes. (6) Running passes. (7) Roll-out passes.

of these spots creates a completely different problem for the defensive linemen who are rushing the passer and for the defensive backs who are covering the receivers.

The ball is thrown with much the same action as a baseball pitcher's "drop ball." Most of the passer's weight is distributed over his right foot as the ball is released from a position just above the ear. Then his weight shifts to his left foot for the follow-through. The passer should never throw when his body is not in balance.

On all long passes, the ball is thrown with a high arch so the receiver can get under it without breaking his speed or stride. On short passes, the ball should be thrown hard at or just below the chest. Then if the ball is fumbled, it will usually fall to the ground and not into the hands of a defender.

Some of the more common deficiencies that the coach should watch for among his passers are:

1. Winding up to throw.
2. Throwing when out of balance.
3. Not following through.
4. Not stepping in the direction of the receiver.
5. Not knowing when to throw hard or soft; high or low.
6. Failing to use the pass protection.
7. Not knowing when and where to lead the receiver.
8. Throwing at the wrong time.

There is no greater heartache in the world than the one suffered by a coach who sees one of his ends break for the sideline in the clear but have to stop to wait for the ball, giving the defensive man time to intercept or knock the pass down. Often these near-completions would have been completed except for a simple mistake on the part of the passer. If the passing game is to be completely successful, the quar-

terback's timing and aim must be perfect, and this requires
work, work, and more work.

The quarterback must never gamble with the football.
When his receivers are not open, the passer should either
become a runner and turn upfield with the ball or throw the
ball out of bounds or just over the receivers. He must never
risk an interception by attempting a completion when his
receivers are not open.

The Receiver

Speed and the ability to utilize that speed at the proper
time are probably the most important traits of the successful pass-receiver. The receiver must be fast and must be
able to control his speed, using it to his advantage to free
himself of defenders at just the right moment.

Other characteristics that are important in pass-receiving
just as in passing are poise, an even temperament, and the
ability to react quickly to defensive changes. The receiver
should know and understand all of the possible defensive
situations and know how to react in any given situation.

And, of course, the receiver must have good hands. It
does him no good to be able to "shake" defenders if he is
not able to catch the ball once it is thrown to him.

Pass-receiving is a very demanding job. Some of the
"musts" that should be stressed by the coach are:

1. The receiver must always run under control, maintaining a pace that will allow him to cut sharply and
   get away from the defensive man.
2. The receiver must run the exact pattern called for.
   If he does not, the passer cannot get the ball to him
   at the proper time and place.

3. The receiver must never take his eyes off the ball once the pass is thrown.
4. The receiver must be an "actor" and not give the pass away.
5. The receiver must never loaf, even when he is not the designated receiver.
6. The receiver must use his body to block out a defender and fight for the ball when there is some question as to who has the right to catch it.

Stanford's all-American end, **Chris Burford,** and quarterback **Dick Norman,** the nation's best passing and receiving combination in 1959.

One of the problems the receiver must face is getting away from a lineman who is trying to hold him up. There are a number of effective techniques that the receiver can use:

1. He can fake a block at the lineman so that the lineman will throw him off.
2. He can drop to one knee and charge out under the defender's hands.
3. He can spin out.
4. He can loosen up from his position, giving himself two ways to break.

PASS PATTERNS

Pass patterns should be designed with only one preferred receiver and never more than two so that the passer has the opportunity to choose his receiver and deliver the ball quickly, thus simplifying the problem of protection. Also, since the quarterback can concentrate on an isolated area and see where the defensive man is, interceptions are less likely.

Diagrammed here are some of the pass patterns that have been used with success at Stanford. It must be emphasized, however, that it is not the number of offensive formations and pass patterns that gives the team a successful passing attack. It is the ability to use a few patterns effectively against the many defenses that the team will have to face.

Right Formation—"Everybody Block" Series

The term "everybody block" means that everybody, with the exception of the two spread men, one end, and the quarterback, is going to block.

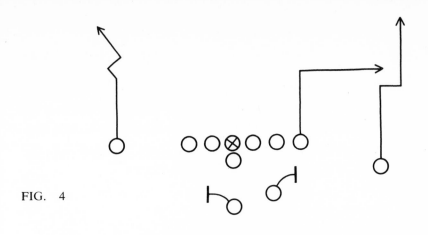

FIG. 4

Sideline to the right end. (See Figure 4.) The flanker runs a sideline-and-up pattern to take the halfback deep. The right end goes ten yards deep and then cuts toward the sideline behind the flanker. The left end "tests" the defensive halfback to see how he covers. The quarterback watches the defensive halfback. If the defense rotates him up to cover the end, the flanker should be open. The flanker must stay wide at all times to avoid the safety.

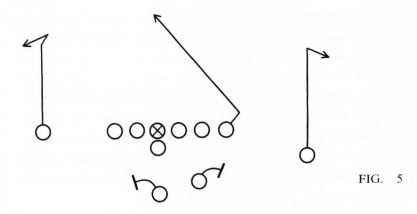

FIG. 5

Sideline to the left end. (See Figure 5.) The flanker runs a deep sideline pattern. The right end sprints through the safety to hold him away from the left side. The left end runs toward the defensive halfback. Fifteen yards past the line,

the end cuts to the sideline, running at a slight angle back
toward the passer. The quarterback fakes the pass to the
inside hook zone just before the end breaks to draw the linebacker to the hook hole. He then leads the end into the
sideline, hitting him about 12 yards deep.

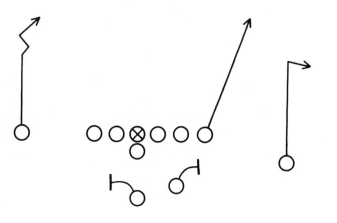

FIG.   6

Flanker sideline. (See Figure 6.) The flanker starts fast
to take the defensive halfback deep but cuts toward the
sideline about fourteen yards past the line, coming back for
the ball. The right end runs between the halfback and safety
so that the halfback will stay deep to cover a possible down-
and-out pattern. The left end runs a "Z" in or out to test
the defensive halfback. The quarterback fakes the pass inside on the flanker's break to help hold the defensive linebacker in the hook zone and then leads the flanker into the
sideline.

Sideline-and-up. (See Figure 7.) The flanker starts fast,
running a sideline pattern, and then goes deep down the
sideline, staying wide in case the safety compensates. The
right end runs through the safety. The left end runs a sideline. The quarterback fakes the sideline pass as the flanker

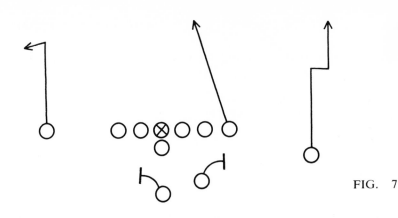

FIG. 7

fakes his sideline move, then hits the flanker soon after he breaks past the defensive halfback.

Left end sideline-and-up. (See Figure 8.) The flanker runs a sideline-and-up and the right end runs a sideline route. The left end starts fast, running a sideline pattern, and then goes deep down the sideline. The quarterback fakes the sideline pass to the flanker, and then hits him as he breaks past the defensive halfback.

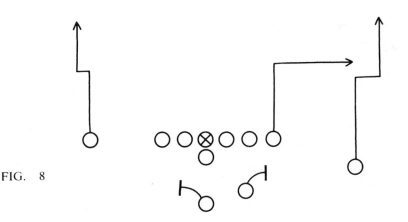

FIG. 8

End across. (See Figure 9.) The flanker runs a deep hook to hold the halfback. The right end clears the line of scrimmage and then cuts to the left corner zone. The left end runs

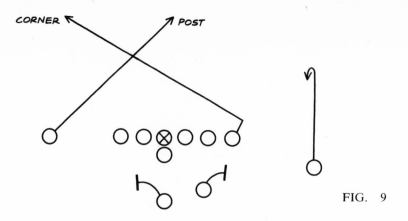

CORNER   POST

FIG. 9

to the deep post zone behind the safety. The quarterback throws to an open receiver.

Right Formation—37 Pass Series

Stop-out. (See Figure 10.) The flanker runs a deep hook. The right end runs through the safety at top speed. The left end runs a deep "in" pattern. The right halfback runs at the defensive linebacker, and then breaks to the sideline. The quarterback fakes to the fullback as on an off-tackle slice play, then throws to either the flanker or right halfback. If the linebacker drops into the hole to cover the hook, the "out" man should be open.

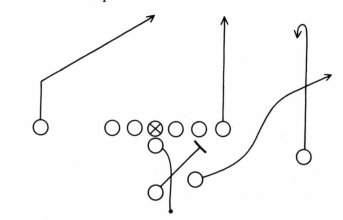

FIG. 10

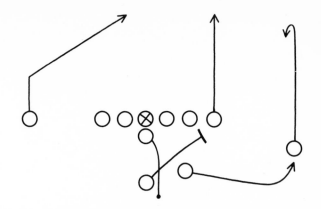

FIG. 11

Stop-swing. (See Figure 11.) The flanker and ends run the same pattern as in the stop-out. The right halfback swings deep enough in the backfield so that he can make the catch and recover before any defenders can get to him. If the linebacker covers the swing man closely, the hook man is then open.

Right end delay center. (See Figure 12.) The flanker and right halfback run the same pattern as in the stop-out. The right end fakes a pass protection block, holding it for three counts, and then sneaks out into the open between the two linebackers. He should be five yards deep or so when the quarterback hits him.

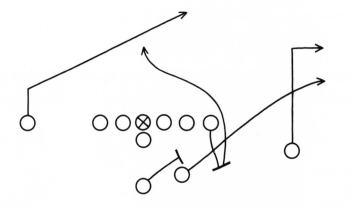

FIG. 12

63

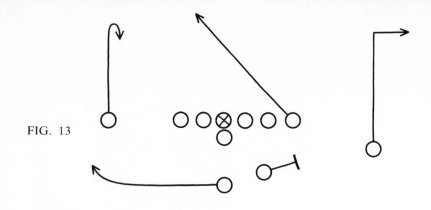

FIG. 13

Split Right Formation

Stop-swing left. (See Figure 13.) The left end runs a stop pattern 12 yards deep. The right end runs through the safety. The flanker runs a quick sideline. The fullback swings left, giving ground so he can catch the ball over his inside shoulder if the ball is thrown to him. The quarterback throws to either the left end or the fullback, depending upon the coverage of the linebacker on that side. The hook man is always open if the linebacker covers the swing man closely.

Stop-out left. (See Figure 14.) The pattern for the stop-out left is the same as that of the stop-swing left, except for the fullback. The fullback goes to the left flat about five yards deep. Again if the linebacker covers the "out" man, the hook is open.

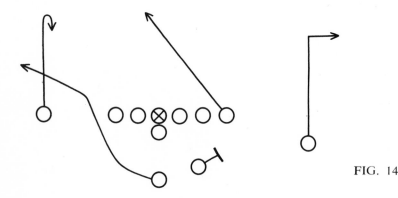

FIG. 14

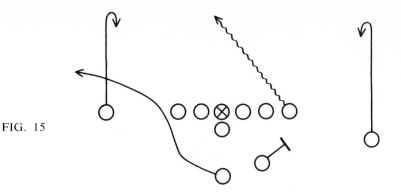

FIG. 15

Stop-out left, right end delay. (See Figure 15.) The right end steps back to protect the passer and then sneaks into the zone between the two linebackers. The end must delay long enough to fool the linebackers. If he makes a good initial pass protection block before crossing the line, the defense is apt to "lose" him.

Running and Jump Passes from Right Formation

39 Running-pass right. (See Figure 16.) The flanker runs a deep corner pattern. The right end steps outside the tackle, goes five yards deep, and then runs parallel to the line of scrimmage. The left end runs through the safety. The quarterback must be prepared to throw or run.

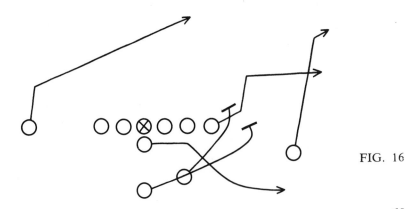

FIG. 16

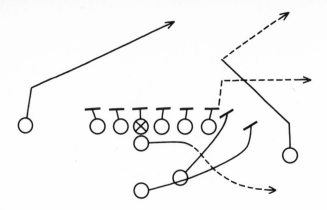

FIG. 17

Jump pass right. (See Figure 17.) The flanker starts down-field to drive the defensive men back, and then cuts in sharp behind the defender at an angle of 45 degrees. The right end blocks hard for three counts, and then runs the same path as on a running pass. The left end runs through the safety. The quarterback stays close to the line and jumps to throw to the flanker. If he is not open, the quarterback rolls out behind the right halfback and fullback. The quarterback then hits either the flanker who is now cutting for the corner or the end in the flat.

Quickie to the right end. (See Figure 18.) The flanker runs a quick sideline. The left end runs through the safety. The right end releases outside the tackle and runs away from the inside linebacker and inside wide linebacker. The quarterback fakes the quick handoff to the right halfback and throws to the right end. If the quarterback sees the safety coming up to help cover, he comes down from the jump to hit the left end who is behind the safety.

FIG. 18

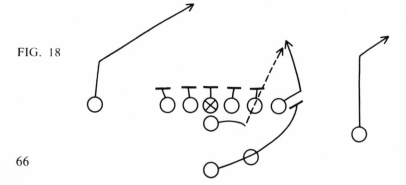

CHAPTER SIX

The Kicking Game

Bobby Dodd
Georgia Tech

BOBBY DODD has posted an enviable record since 1945 when he became head football coach at Georgia Tech. His teams have won 128 games, while losing only 50, have won eight major bowl games, and have produced sixteen all-Americans.

Dodd's 1951-56 squads provided the six most fabulous years in Tech's football-rich history, logging an overall 59-7-3 record, including six consecutive bowl victories. Following Tech's brilliant 1952 season, which included an 11-0 season record and a 24-7 win over Mississippi in the Sugar Bowl, Dodd was voted College Coach of the Year.

After graduation from Kingsport, Tennessee, High School where he was an 83-pound terror at quarterback and end, Dodd enrolled at the University of Tennessee to begin an athletic career that has become a legend in the South. With Dodd at quarterback, the Vols romped through three seasons, losing only one game during those three years. For his outstanding play, Dodd was named all-Southern in 1928 and 1929 and all-American in 1930.

Recognized as an expert on all phases of football, Dodd is author of a very well-received coaching book, *Bobby Dodd on Football*. (Prentice-Hall, Inc., Englewood Cliffs, N. J., 1954.)

The Kicking Game

One of the most important elements of winning football is the kicking game. I don't think anyone can put too much emphasis on this phase of football. Although it may not be as dramatic as running or passing, kicking, either directly or indirectly, decides the issue in practically every close game.

Too often the kicking game is pushed back into a less important role as if it was just something you "have to have" to play football. How many coaches, for example, include every phase of the kicking game in their practice schedule from the first week of training?

It is easy to overlook the kicking game because so much of the yardage on kicks is concealed. A part of the statistics kept for each game should include yardage of kicks, punts returned, and kickoffs returned—both offensively and defensively, in addition to the net distance of each actual kick. A coach who keeps these statistics for his team will soon realize how important the kicking game is.

THE PUNT

Almost any well-coordinated athlete can learn to punt a football well enough to come within four or five yards of his target. Such a punter comprises an offense in himself. His punts may be planned to gain ground, to penetrate the enemy territory, or to put pressure on opponents when the ball must be surrendered to them. This is "concealed yardage" which will always figure prominently in any close ball game.

The punter can develop a high degree of efficiency and consistency if he works on certain elementary fundamentals. Some boys are naturals and require very little coaching. When you find a boy who is unorthodox in style but still gets distance and accuracy, do not make the mistake of trying to change him. You cannot improve on results, and performance is all you are striving for.

Dropping the Ball

If the ball is held and dropped differently by the kicker each time, it will react differently each time. If it is dropped and handled with a uniform release, it will tend to react similarly each time. So it follows that the kicker must adopt a standard manner of holding the ball if he is to be consistent with his kicking.

The best way to hold the ball is to place it in the right hand with the middle finger resting along the line of the bottom seam. Make sure the hand is forward enough to have control of the ball.

The left hand merely serves as a guide and should be placed very lightly against the front left side of the ball. Make sure the left hand doesn't exert any pressure, since this will cause the ball to fall out of the line of release.

Have the punter work on dropping the ball many times before he even tries to punt it. A perfectly dropped ball will usually bounce backward after hitting the ground.

Body Balance

Body balance is *the* prerequisite for a good punter. He must be relaxed and in balance.

A right-footed kicker usually has a definite "drift" to the right, and a left-footed kicker usually "drifts" to the left.

Dave Davis, one of Tech's all-time great punters.

Johnny Menger, another of Georgia Tech's great punters.

This "drift" can be cut to a minimum by a slight correction in stance.

Never let a punter kick without thinking: "Am I in the middle, punting for distance?" "Am I kicking from either hash mark or kicking for the 'coffin corner'?" A punter kicks under different circumstances every time, and he must always be conscious of this difference or he will not be able to punt with intelligence before a crowd.

Never let a boy get the idea that he can punt better by leaving the ground with his balanced foot. He *may* do this naturally and do a good job. If so, certainly don't change him—but it is contrary to standard punting form. No one has complete control over the ball if he is in the air. For perfect control, the foot on which the kicker balances should be kept on the ground.

Stance

The punter's feet should be about six inches apart with the right foot slightly ahead. He should stand in a relaxed manner with the knees slightly flexed, arms extended, and hands open, ready for the snap from center. This gives the center a good target, and it gives the punter good position in case he has to go after a bad snap.

The punter must always be prepared for a bad snap. If a bad snap comes on any down other than the fourth, he must be prepared to pick up the ball and run, rather than try a delayed kick from an awkward position. If it is fourth down, he must be prepared to get the ball off no matter where the ball is centered.

Steps

After receiving the ball, the punter should take a short step with his front foot and then follow with a full step on the balanced foot. The kicking foot then comes forward and up for contact with the ball. This is the common step-and-a-half form. Some coaches call it the "hop, step, kick" style, which is a variation of the step-and-a-half, but is a little quicker and covers a little less ground.

Acceleration and Contact

After the second full step, the kicking leg starts gaining momentum. The leg, slightly bent, locks and swings into the ball with the toe pointing downward to create a spiral. The ball is released as close to the foot as possible.

Follow-through

The follow-through is important in every phase of athletics and has a definite place in punting. Following-through helps to insure that the ball will reach its objective. Drawing back the arms to the hip adds to the effectiveness of the follow-through.

PROTECTING AND COVERING THE PUNT

Punt protecting is a vital part of a team's practice and must be put in the practice schedule and worked on—both dummy and at full speed. Too many coaches work on trick plays and naked reverses before they ever work on this important phase of the game.

Punt protection is easy for a coach to overlook because ball games are never won directly through punt protection. But rest assured there is no quicker way to *lose* a game than to have a punt blocked or partially blocked.

There are two basic types of punt protection. Since each type has its place, every coach should include both in his coaching. The two basic types are *spread protection* and *tight protection*.

Spread Protection

The one great advantage that the "spread" has over the "tight" is the better coverage of the punt. However, there is one important thing that must be considered before using spread protection: *You must have a center who can snap the ball at least fourteen yards with some degree of accuracy.* If you cannot find a boy who can do this, spread protection is eliminated automatically.

Spread Punt Protection Line Up

To give the team more speed and better coverage where it is needed, the guards and tackles switch places and the halfbacks line up outside the ends. (See Figure 19.)

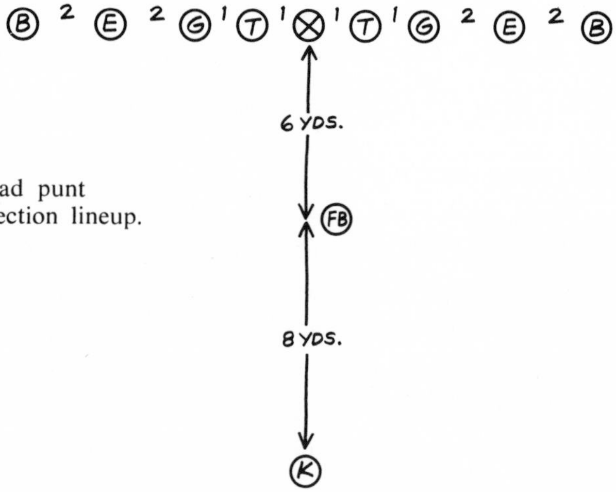

FIG. 19   Spread punt
            protection lineup.

The *center* takes his position first. Then the tackles take a one-yard split from the center; the *guards* line up with a one-yard split from the tackles. (The distance between the center and guards and between the guards and tackles is one man-space.)

The *ends* line up with a two-yard split from the guards; the *halfbacks* line up with a two-yard split from the ends. (Having the halfbacks on the line gives far better coverage than if they are in the backfield.)

The *fullback's* job is to protect the kicker's foot. He lines up six yards deep with his left foot keyed on the center's right foot—just room enough for the ball to clear. He blocks the first man who comes through.

The *kicker* is lined up at least fourteen yards from the ball.

Drill for Position

Here is a good drill to get each player conscious of his relative position. Select a part of the field and mark off each man's position accurately with a circle the size of his offensive base. Work on punt protection and coverage until the players unconsciously take their accurate positions. Don't let them cut down their splits.

Blocking Responsibilities for Spread Punt

The *center* is not responsible for a block. His first and only responsibility is to get off a good snap to the kicker. He leaves on the snap to cover the punt.

The linemen's rule in the spread punt formation is INSIDE, OVER, OUTSIDE. All linemen have inside responsibility first, making sure that they protect the gap to their inside before they consider blocking a man who is over them or to their outside.

The *fullback* lines up in position to protect the kicker's foot, providing the punter's only protection in the back-field. He blocks the first man that comes into his area, stepping forward or to the outside. This is an important as-signment. A mistake here can lead to a blocked kick.

The coach should spend a lot of time in developing the actual "clock" speed of his kickers. From the spread punt formation no more than 2.2 to 2.8 seconds should be taken from the time the ball is snapped until it is punted. The cen-ter's snap should be 1.0 to 1.2 seconds and the kicking time no more than 1.2 to 1.6 seconds.

Another factor to be considered is the amount of time the ball will be in the air. On a 40-yard kick, the ball should reach the safety man's hands in four seconds. A medium-timed kick (2.5 seconds) of 40 yards thus leaves the team with 6.5 seconds to block and run 40 yards. Since approxi-mately one second is needed for spread punt blocking, the team has 5.5 seconds for covering the punt.

Covering From Spread Punt Protection

(See Figure 20.)

The *halfbacks* leave on the snap and cover fast to the out-side in the first wave.

The *ends* check to their inside and then cover in the sec-ond wave.

The *guards* protect their responsibility and cover from this position. They may be in the first or second wave.

The *tackles* protect their responsibility and cover in the second wave.

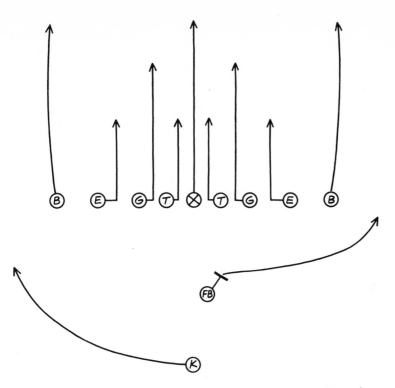

FIG. 20   Covering from spread punt formation.

The *center* leaves on the snap and goes for the ball. He
   may be in the first or second wave.
The *fullback* protects his responsibility and covers right.
The *punter* covers left.

Tight Punt Protection

"Tight" punt protection should be a part of every offense.
It is needed when kicking from the goal line where the
punter cannot get his required depth of fourteen yards for
the spread protection. There will also be days when weather
factors will make it very hazardous for the center to snap
the ball fourteen yards. When you need tight protection,
you *really* need it.

From the tight punt formation, no more than 1.8 to 2.2
seconds should be taken to get the kick away. The center's
snap should be .6 to .8 seconds and the kicking time 1.2
to 1.4 seconds.

Tight Protection Line Up

In the tight punt formation, a cup is formed by eight men
who are responsible for the area from their outside foot to
the outside foot of the man to their inside. (See Figure 21.)
The punter is responsible for kicking over the protection.

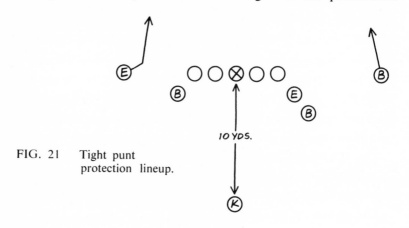

FIG. 21   Tight punt
           protection lineup.

Individual Protection Responsibility

The center's first responsibility is to get a good snap of
the ball to the punter; then he is responsible for his own
base. He must not leave too soon and create a gap for delayed rushers trying to block the kick. *A safe rule is for all
linemen to delay two seconds before leaving.*

The *guards* and *tackles* take a normal base with about a twelve-inch split. Don't allow them to close the gap to their inside. If the guards or tackles cut down on their base or split, they automatically cut down the protected kicking zone. On the snap of the ball the guards and tackles broaden their base and at the same time shift their inside foot forward with a quick stagger of both feet. Their position should be a low crouch because they are waiting passively to absorb the charge of the defense. They must *not* be aggressive—that is the way gaps are created.

The guards and tackles should never move more than one foot at a time after taking position until *after* the two-second interval. Their responsibility is first to the inside. If no one comes inside, the guards and tackles must be alert for overloading the zone to the outside and be ready to, secondly, help out outside by moving only the outside foot. Interior linemen should always strive to keep their base parallel to the line of scrimmage.

The right end and right back line up at a 45-degree angle to the line of scrimmage. They should take a base that is as wide and comfortable as possible, with knees slightly flexed and head up. Their first responsibility is inside, and they should never move more than one foot at a time. Look for stunts or overloading in this zone. The end must be ready to help out if the loaded zone is between him and the right back. He can help by taking a step with the outside foot and by snapping the elbow up level with the shoulder to give more blocking base. The right end and right back have the most important jobs in this protection since they are directly in front of and protecting the kicking zone.

The *left back* lines up at a 45-degree angle to the line of scrimmage in a position where he can touch the left offensive tackle's hip. His responsibility is similar to that of the right end, but he does not have to help outside. He maintains his base, forcing anyone who is rushing the kicker to go to the outside, so that they must run in an arc to get to the kicking zone. The rusher must never be allowed to reach the kicker's foot by going in a straight line.

The *left end* lines up with a two-yard split from the offensive left tackle. When punting on fourth down, he should move in and bump the defensive end before releasing to cover the punt. On anything other than fourth down punting situations, he releases for coverage as soon as the ball is snapped.

The *wingback* lines up eight to twelve yards from the offensive tackle and leaves on the snap.

The *kicker* must be aware of the protected zone. If he wants to kick to his left, he must move over to the right to compensate for his kicking zone. *Each member of the team should realize the zone he is protecting.*

Covering the Tight Protection

(See Figure 22.)

From tackle to tackle the line protects for two seconds and then fans out to protect the width of the field.

The *right end* covers outside in the second wave.

The *left end* covers outside in the first wave.

The *right back* covers quickly to the outside in the second wave.

The *left back* covers outside in the second wave.

The *wingback* goes for the ball, without any outside responsibility, in the first wave.

The *punter* covers to his left.

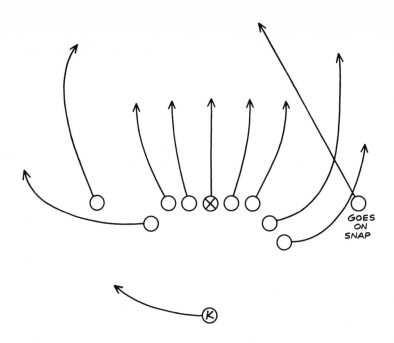

FIG. 22   Covering from tight punt protection.

THE QUICK KICK

The quick kick is one of the most effective weapons a team can use. The value of the quick kick lies in the element of surprise. It can get a team out of a hole and put the other team in one.

For best results the kick should be low and end-over-end. Usually it is advisable to quick kick *away* from the safety man as well as over his head.

Mechanics of the Quick Kick

Taking a low lead-pass from the center, the kicker turns to his right, takes a short step with his right foot and a full step with his left, and drives off his balanced foot. His steps are parallel to the line of scrimmage. Swinging his kicking foot in an arc and turning his body, he strikes the ball on the rear third, giving it the end-over-end movement that brings about a long roll. The ball should be held very lightly with the left and right hands at each end.

A kick of this type will usually catch the safety man going to his left, and the kick can be very easily and naturally kicked to his right. This kick is easy to coach and will get the needed results.

The other type of quick kick that can be employed is the "rocker step." The kicker assumes his normal backfield stance and receives the ball from the center at the knee of his kicking leg. Taking a short step back with his left foot and a full step forward with the same foot, he kicks the ball end-over-end by dropping the ball evenly on the top of his foot.

Protecting the Quick Kick

There are a number of methods for protecting the quick kick, but generally the blocking should all be aggressive along the line of scrimmage. These blocks will keep the defenses low and therefore protect the low flight of the ball

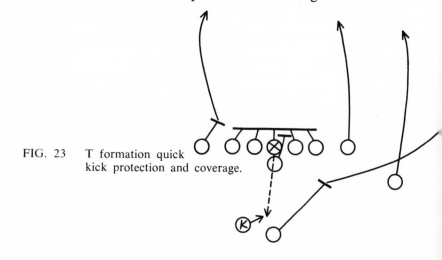

FIG. 23   T formation quick
kick protection and coverage.

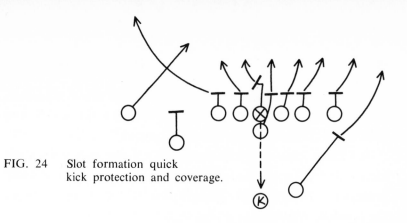

FIG. 24   Slot formation quick
kick protection and coverage.

over the line. Quick coverage must be stressed to take full
advantage of the kick. (See Figures 23 and 24.)

Covering the Quick Kick

On a quick kick as on a normal punt, stress the importance of covering as fast as possible. When an opposing
team has to start in the danger zone after receiving a quick
kick, subsequent breaks will often set up a score for you.
Go back and find out who made the tackle on the kick and
give him credit for making the touchdown possible. In this
way you build up a sense of the relative importance of covering the kick with as much speed as possible.

FIELDING AND RETURNING THE PUNT

Fielding. There is no set form for handling and returning
punts, but certain fundamentals will help to guide you in
coaching the men who field punts:

1. *They must study the punter in each game.* Get all the
information you can on his kicking habits. This will help
the safety man to line up correctly.

2. *They should always be conscious of the wind and
weather conditions and what effect these conditions will
have on the punt.*

3. *They should keep their eyes on the ball at all times.*
By split vision they can decide if making a fair catch is a
possibility. They must concentrate on catching the ball first.

4. *They should break the flight of the ball with their
hands and bring the ball into their chest.* Once in complete
possession, the receiver changes the ball from his chest to
the hand in which he is going to carry the ball.

When working on the fielding of punts, have your safety
men handle punts inside the 20-yard line. They must know
when to let the ball go and when they are justified in fielding the ball in this zone. A good general rule to apply is:
A punt should never be fielded inside the 10-yard line. The
only exception would be in the case of a quick kick or punt
over the safety man's head on which the punter has out-
kicked his coverage.

The only way to be sure of no mistakes in the 20-yard
area is to spend a lot of practice time fielding punts in this
area. There are just as many chances for bad breaks in other
areas of the field, but they are not as noticeable since they
are never as costly.

Work punters and safety men as a group, letting the punters kick high for the 10-yard line or angle for the "coffin
corner" and the safety men practice fielding the punts.

Punt Returns

When it is executed well, the prettiest play in football is
a sideline punt return that goes all the way. It is relatively
simple to add to the practice schedule and is well worth the
time and effort.

First, sell the boys on the idea that they are going to return the punt all the way—that once the safety man hits
the sideline, he should go for the touchdown. The blockers

must be conscious of timing their blocks according to the length, height, and direction of the punt. Usually, the first man down in the wall will be the key blocker, and all of the others will be timing their blocks on him. His responsibility should be to allow the runner to hit the sideline.

Individual Responsibilities

The following responsibilities are for a 6-3-2 alignment with the return up the right sideline. For a left sideline return, the assignments are simply reversed.

The *right end* lines up nose-on with the left offensive end. He delays the end from covering the kick as long as possible, then sprints for the sideline. When he is about 10 yards from the sideline, he turns at a right angle and goes straight down the field. If the end is sure that the ball-carrier can get to the sideline without having to move over into the center of the field, he makes his block at about 10 yards from the sideline. If the ball should be kicked to the opposite side of the field, he may have to come over to pick up the runner. He then positions himself and takes the first man to the inside in this zone.

The *right tackle* lines up head-on with the left offensive tackle. His play is the same as the right end's, except that he will space himself approximately seven to eight yards from the end and will block the first men to the inside in this zone.

The *right guard* and the *left guard* line up on the offensive guards and carry out the same responsibility. If any of the men in the wall find no one in their zone to block, they should look to the inside to see if anyone has filtered through the wall. If anyone has come through, the guards should block them out.

The *left end* and *left tackle* line up on the outside shoulder of the right end and right tackle respectively. They rush hard and try to force the kick down the middle. The left tackle goes on into the sideline and becomes part of the wall. The left end comes over and remains on the line of scrimmage and is the "safety valve." He takes the last man, who is usually the kicker.

The *right halfback* gets an outside position on the left offensive end and "dogs" him from the outside to keep him away from the exchange or fake of the ball. He then blocks him, being sure to make the block at the right time.

The *center* sprints to position himself on the left offensive end from the inside. After the right halfback has blocked the end, the center should clean up and put him on the ground again. This is the key block and should enable the runner to get inside the wall.

The *fullback* comes over quickly in front of the ball and takes the first man to come into this zone. His responsibility is to protect the exchange or fake of the ball.

Exchange and Fake of the Ball

The twin safeties have a primary responsibility in the execution of an exchange. They must be "actors." The way they carry out their fakes will largely determine the success of the return. They must always keep about 15 yards between them. They cannot fool the men covering the punt if they are too close together and make the exchange too soon, giving the men covering time to adjust. If the ball is kicked between them, the one who fields the punt should give ground, if necessary, to keep this distance.

The one who fields the punt always goes in front. This shields the keep or exchange better. The ball carrier should retreat, if necessary, to hit the corridor formed by the wall of blockers.

Double Safety Sideline Return

The correct maneuver for the double safety sideline return is shown in Figure 25.

Drill for Sideline Punt Return

The sideline return needs a lot of dummy work to practice timing position and blocks with the keep or exchange. This dummy work can be used for a running drill to end practice:

FIG. 25   Double safety sideline return, right.

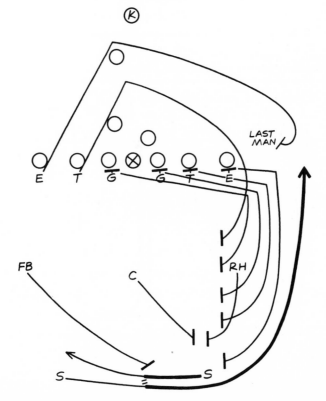

Put two dummies about 10 yards from each sideline on the line of scrimmage. With this set up, work the exchange both left and right, making the men in the wall go around these dummies. It is very important in the return that the men who form the wall do not cut the corner.

Double Safety Middle Return

The middle return helps the sideline return in that it keeps the covering team "honest" in playing the sideline return.

FIG. 26   Double safety middle return.

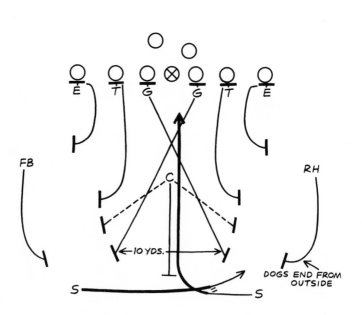

Individual Responsibilities

The *guards* line up on the offensive guards, delay them as long as possible, and then sprint across to a position in front of the exchange or keep of the ball. They try to form a lane about 10 yards wide down the middle of the field. The guards will be the first men in the wall and should take the first man to the outside in their zone.

The *tackles* line up head-on with the offensive tackles, delay them as long as possible, and then swing to the inside and position themselves eight to 10 yards from the guards, blocking the first man in their zone.

The *ends* have the same responsibility as the tackles. If no one comes into their zone, the ends should then look into the lane and take anyone in the middle.

The *fullback* positions himself outside the offensive right end and "dogs" him from the outside to help protect the keep or exchange.

The *right halfback* has the same responsibility as the left offensive end.

The center is allowed to vary his responsibility, particularly if the team covering is trying to use him as a key to determine quickly the direction of the sideline return. The center may drop straight back and protect the exchange or block either end covering the kick.

Exchange or Keep

The exchange or keep for the middle return is the same as the sideline return except that the corridor is now up the middle instead of along the sideline. The twin safeties must always remember to keep distance between them.

A safe rule for the middle return is: *The one who fields the punt always keeps and never exchanges.*

Single Safety Sideline Return Against Tight Protection

(See Figure 27.)

The *right end* lines up nose-on with the left offensive end, delays his covering of the punt, and then swings to the sideline and becomes the first man in the wall.

The *right tackle* delays the left back, then swings to the sideline into the wall, spacing himself seven or eight yards from the end.

FIG. 27   Single safety sideline return against tight protection.

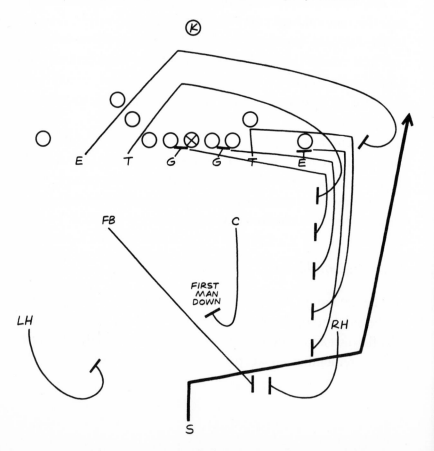

The *right guard* drives hard into the gap between the left offensive tackle and the left offensive guard. If he drives for quick penetration, he should be able to force both men to block him and thereby delay the coverage.

The *left guard* drives similarly into the gap between the center and the offensive right guard, then swings over and becomes part of the wall.

The *left end* and *left tackle* rush hard on the inside to try to force the kick down the middle. The tackle then goes into the wall, and the end remains on the line of scrimmage to pick off the last man.

The *fullback* crosses quickly to the other side of the field to help the right halfback double-team the left offensive end.

The *center* drops back and takes the first man down on his side. He should time his block to allow the safety man to come back up the middle before swinging to the sideline.

The *right halfback* blocks the right end out.

The *safety man* should bring the ball up the middle and then hit the sideline between the blocks of the fullback and center.

THE PLACE KICK

Any boy who has "snap" in his leg may become a fine place kicker, but he must have patience and be willing to pay the price of hard practice. Place kicking takes practice, practice, and *more* practice—until it becomes mechanical.

Make a 'T'

Place kickers should always kick from a 'T'—either real or drawn on the ground. Any sort of 'T' is satisfactory, so long as it eliminates the goal posts as a factor in the kick.

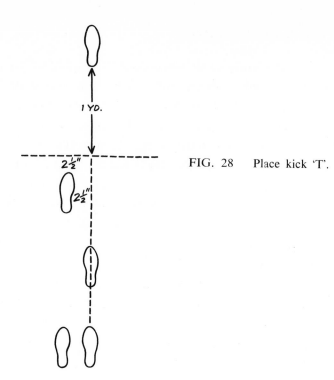

FIG. 28   Place kick 'T'.

The 'T' can help the place kicker in the following ways:
1. It lines up the kick.
2. It helps develop kicking "straight through."
3. It allows the kicker to check his non-kicking foot's position at the time of the kick. This foot must always step in the same place.

The kicker can never develop accuracy unless he keeps his steps and foot position the same each time he kicks.

Form

Form for the place kicker is as follows:
1. Step with the kicking foot.
2. Step with the left foot about two and a half inches away from both lines of the 'T'.
3. Begin the swing of the kicking foot, making sure that the swing does not start too far from the ball. Lock

the knee to get the needed "snap" and create a pen-
dulum from the hip. Kick *through* the ball and finish in front of the 'T' with the third step.

4. Finish the swing and the kick, keeping head down
    and body slightly bent, and watching the foot go into
    the ball. Eyes should remain on the 'T' until the kick
    is completed. We tell our kickers that they needn't
    watch to see if the kick is good or not. The officials
    will let us know.

If the kicker is slicing the ball, the coach can show him
where he is hitting the ball by putting some chalk on the toe
of his shoe. After the kick, the coach can examine the ball
and show the kicker exactly where he is hitting the ball.

Some Aids in Developing a Good Place Kicker
1. Eliminate all preliminary movements before the kick.
2. Always use the same movements.
3. Never kick when the leg is tired.
4. Start the kick when the ball hits the holder's hands.
5. Kick a spot on the 'T' and not the ball.

The Holder

The ball-holder is important, but not as important as is
often thought. With proper form the place kicker can kick
almost any ball from the 'T' through the goal posts, regardless of how the ball is held.

The holder should line up seven yards from the line of
scrimmage with both knees on the ground. His hands should
be outstretched in front of his chest to give the center a
target. Do not let the holder give the target over the 'T'.
This is an awkward and dangerous position to handle a
snap that is not directly into his hands. The holder deter-

mines when the ball should be snapped. He asks the kicker if he is ready, and then gives a set signal for the offensive line.

Protection of the Place Kicker

Protection for the place kicker is passive blocking for everyone on the line of scrimmage, including the two backs. Everyone is responsible for the area from his outside foot to the outside foot of the first man to his inside. This is commonly referred to as "cup protection," and any rush must come from the outside. (See Figure 29.)

From end to end this protection can be best carried out by shifting the inside foot to a forward position and at the same time broadening the base with the outside foot. A low crouch to make a low block will tend to lower the defensive charge. The offensive line should not know when the ball is going to be snapped. This will help keep them from being aggressive on their initial charge.

Protecting for the extra point or field goal will be a relatively simple matter if no one is aggressive or leaves his initial zone. If someone does, a gap will be created for the defensive men to penetrate. If the two outside backs will retain their base and force any rush *outside* of their position, the kick will be gotten off.

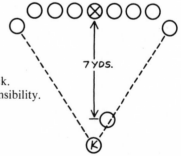

FIG. 29   Protection of the place kick.
Everyone has inside responsibility.

THE FIELD GOAL

The field goal, of course, is similar to the extra point. It is a valuable weapon and very often is as good as a touchdown. If there is a good place kicker on the team, determine his range on field goals and keep this in mind. Let the team know it will be used when the occasion presents itself.

Protection for the field goal is the same as for the extra point. The only difference is that the holder may have to vary his position slightly on bad kicking angles to insure kicking inside the protection. The kicker will adjust the angle of the 'T' to the goal post.

THE KICK OFF

Form for the kick off is basically the same as for the place kick. The kicker places the ball on the tee, slanting it back at a slight angle, and measures off the proper distance for his approach. This distance will vary from kicker to kicker, but each man must find out the number of steps that he will need in order to reach full momentum without breaking stride. The same distance should be used for every kick.

Covering the Kick Off

The fastest, best-tackling men should be put at the ends of the line. (These will usually be backfield men.) Send them for the ball without any outside responsibilities.

Next in position should be the ends; they flare to the outside and are responsible for any sideline return. Usually, the ends have this same type of responsibility on defense, so the team will tend to have better coverage from this lineup.

The covering alignment of the rest of the personnel is not

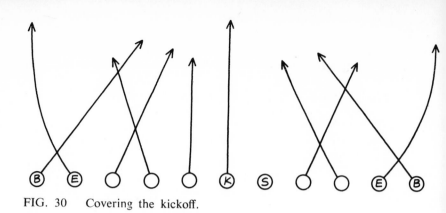

FIG. 30   Covering the kickoff.

too important, but try to keep some sort of balance. Don't have all of the slower men or the best tacklers on one side. Try to space them alternately.

The kicker covers, and the safety man remains on the 35-yard line and is exactly what the name implies. He should be the man who is the regular safety in a defensive set-up.

Once you line up a set from end to end, keep it constant. Be sure that any substitutes in the middle know their correct positions. If you are sure an opponent is returning kick offs by numbering the kick off team, occasionally let the third and fourth men cross and switch assignments. This may help to confuse blocking assignments.

Everyone except the kicker should line up on the 35-yard line facing the inside. When the kicker reaches the 35-yard line, the rest of the team should move ahead one step behind him, watch him kick the ball, and cover. (See Figure 30.)

No one should ever be off-side on the kick off. This is an unpardonable sin.

KICK OFF RETURNS

Line up five men in the restraining zone at least two yards past the 40-yard line. To insure a legal formation, do not let them take a step back until the ball has been kicked.

The *ends* are normally lined up on the 25-yard line about 15 yards in from the sideline.

96

The *fullback* is lined up in the middle of the field on the 20-yard line.

The *halfbacks* are lined up about 15 yards from the sideline at about the five-yard line.

The *safety man* should be on the goal line, in position to field any bouncing ball or short kick. If a kicker is consistently a short kicker, everyone should adjust by moving up accordingly.

Sideline Kick Off Return

A power sideline return with double blocks on the key men should carry to at least the 35-yard line. The return is not designed to go all the way.

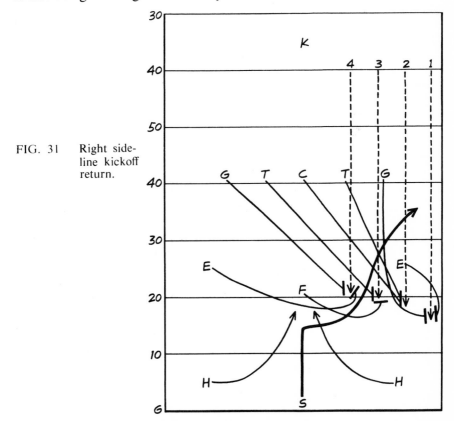

FIG. 31   Right sideline kickoff return.

Number the kick off team by counting in from the side-line. (See Figure 31.)

The *left guard* and *left end* double-team the No. 4 man from the sideline.

The *left tackle* and *fullback* double-team the No. 3 man.

The *center* and *right tackle* double-team the No. 2 man and try to take him out.

The *right end* and *right guard* take the No. 1 man and block him out.

The *left halfback* sprints to get ahead of the safety man and takes the first man to show.

The *right halfback* swings inside and to the middle and is personal interference for the safety man.

The *safety man* starts up the middle and then swings to the sideline between the No. 2 and No. 3 men of the kick off team.

In any return of any kick, timing of blocks is by far the most important thing. A well-timed, poor block is better than a good block which is poorly timed.

Middle Kick Off Return

Number the three men on each side of the kicker, start-ing from the inside. (See Figure 32.)

The *left guard* takes the No. 2 man on his side.

The *left tackle* takes the No. 1 man on the opposite side.

The *center* takes the kicker. Give him the option of go-ing up quickly to take the kicker or of dropping back and timing his block with the rest of the team.

The *right guard* takes the No. 2 man on his side.

The *right tackle* takes the No. 1 man on the opposite side.

The *ends* take the No. 3 men on their sides of the field.

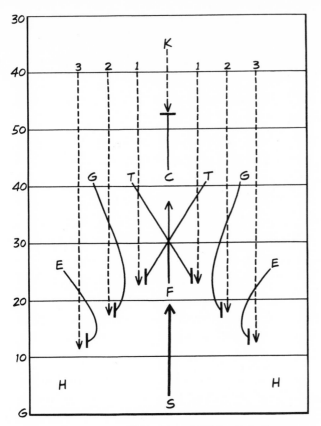

FIG. 32   Middle kickoff return.

The *fullback* drops back and is personal interference for the safety man.

The *halfbacks* sprint to get ahead of the ball carrier and line up on the fullback; the three men form a wedge until forced to leave to block.

The *safety man* stays behind the wedge, forcing the kick off team to come to the wedge. He should get as much distance as possible before going on his own.

CHAPTER SEVEN

Tennessee's
Single Wing Offense

Bowden Wyatt
University of Tennessee

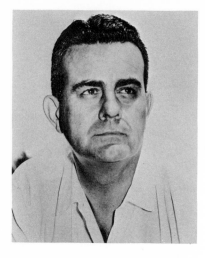

BOWDEN WYATT was small and unheralded as a high school football player, but his ambition had always been to play at the University of Tennessee under perfectionist General Bob Neyland. Through hard work, great devotion to physical conditioning, and eagerness to learn more about the game, Wyatt readily established himself as one of the finest ends in Tennessee history, winning all-American honors in 1938.

After lifting football to new heights at Wyoming and Arkansas, Wyatt returned to his alma mater in 1955 as head coach of the Volunteers. At Wyoming, he established his reputation as a builder of well-conditioned, fundamentally sound football teams as he pulled the Cowboys from the depths of the Skyline Conference to the championship. At Arkansas, Wyatt repeated himself by leading a team that was not supposed to win a game to the Southwest Conference title and a Cotton Bowl berth.

When Wyatt's Tennessee team won the Southeastern Conference championship in 1956, he became the only collegiate coach ever to win championships in three major conferences. Following the 1956 season, Wyatt was presented with the Coach of the Year award in recognition of his many coaching achievements.

Tennessee's Single Wing Offense

Although very few schools are now using the single wing-back offense, we at Tennessee firmly believe in it as an effective basic formation. There are a number of reasons for our believing in the single wing as we do:

1. Because of the years spent with the single wing at Tennessee, we feel that we know and understand it better than any of the other formations.

2. The single wing has been very good to us and has consistently produced results over the years.

3. The single wing coach has one big advantage over most of his opponents. Since most teams use variations of the T formation, opponents of the single wing must attempt to stop a formation which they have not been playing against every week. Our opponents usually have only one week to change their defenses in order to cope with our offense.

THE SINGLE WING LINEUP

When our players leave the huddle, they line up in one of two formations—either formation right or formation left. Our players are not called right end and left end, right tackle and left tackle, etc. Rather, they are referred to as strong-side end and weak-side end, strong-side tackle and weak-side tackle, strong-side guard and weak-side guard. In formation right, the strong-side linemen are on the right side of the line. In formation left, they are on the left side.

103

The backfield men are the wingback, fullback, blocking back, and tailback. Figure 33 illustrates the positions of the players when they are in formation right.

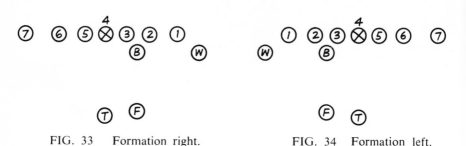

FIG. 33   Formation right.   FIG. 34   Formation left.

In our left formation, the linemen that were on the right side of the line take positions on the left side, and linemen that were on the left side of the line take positions on the right side. (See Figure 34.) The number 1, number 2, and number 3 men are always our strong-side linemen, and numbers 5, 6, and 7 are always our weak-side linemen.

The backfield men retain their relative positions, too, in the change from formation right to formation left. In our left formation, the wingback becomes the left formation wingback, the blocking back remains the blocking back, the fullback is still the fullback, and the tailback continues as the tailback.

Lining up the team in this manner when going from one formation to the other cuts the players' assignments by one-half. When a play is run from formation right, each player has a definite assignment. Then when the team goes into formation left and runs the same play to the opposite side, each player has the same assignment, except that any blocks must be made with the opposite shoulder. Turning the entire team around requires each player to learn only half as many assignments as he would if we did not turn the team

John Majors, all-American tailback at Tennessee.

around. This reduction in the number of assignments that must be learned facilitates the teaching of our offense and gives us an advantage over teams that use other formations.

The Single Wing Line

At Tennessee, a balanced line is used, with varying splits. (See Figure 35.) The strong-side end's split is determined by the type of defense we are playing against. He takes an eighteen-inch split if it is an odd defense and a twenty-four

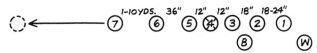

FIG. 35   Line splits.

inch split against an even defense. The strong-side tackle is split eighteen inches from the strong-side guard. The guard is split twelve inches from the center.

On the weak side of the line, the guard takes a twelve-inch split from the center, the tackle is thirty-six inches from the guard, and the end is split out from one to ten yards, depending upon the type of play that is being run.

The Single Wing Backfield

The positions that the backs take in the backfield vary slightly according to particular assignments.

The wingback usually positions himself as close to the line of scrimmage as the rules will permit, although on some

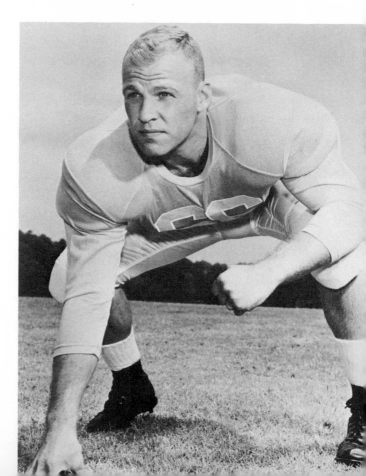

plays he is a little deeper. Since he is primarily a blocker, the wingback normally lines up as close as he can to the man he is to block.

The blocking back takes a position anywhere from directly behind the strong-side guard to directly behind the strong-side tackle.

The tailback lines up four to six yards deep in the backfield and directly behind the center.

The fullback lines up directly behind the gap between the strong-side guard and tackle. He may be anywhere from eighteen inches deeper than the tailback to a yard nearer the line of scrimmage.

The wingback must first be a blocker, then a passer or pass receiver, and very occasionally a ball carrier.

The blocking back blocks for the ball carrier and once in a while handles the ball on buck laterals and option plays.

The tailback is the versatile member of the single wing backfield. He must be able to run, pass, and kick the ball.

The fullback must be able to make the inside and outside blocks on the defensive end and to run the ball on trap and wedge plays.

SINGLE WINGBACK PLAYS

The four series of single wing plays used at Tennessee are the straight series, buck-lateral series, draw series, and tailback-spin.

Straight Series

Off-tackle play to the strong side. The tailback takes a direct snap from center with a step-and-a-half lead to the strong side. On his third step, the tailback makes a head-

ill Johnson, all-American guard at Tennessee.

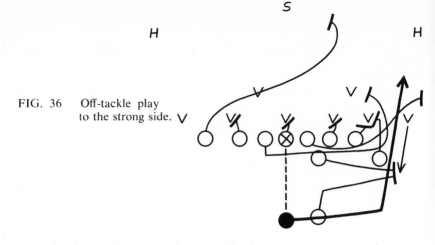

FIG. 36   Off-tackle play
                to the strong side.

and-shoulders fake to the outside in an attempt to draw
the defensive end across the line of scrimmage. He then
cuts inside the end. (See Figure 36.)

The fullback and blocking back drive shoulder to shoulder at the defensive end, taking him toward the sideline. The
wingback and strong-side end take the defensive tackle in.

The strong-side and weak-side guards pull out of the line
and lead the play through the hole. The strong-side guard
blocks to the outside of the hole. The weak-side guard blocks
to the inside.

Off-tackle play to the weak side. If opponents rotate their
defenses to the strong side, the offense may have more success with the off-tackle play to the weak side.

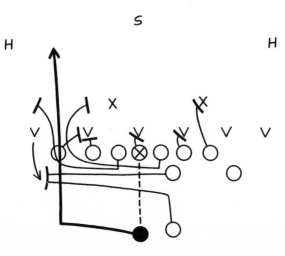

FIG. 37
Off-tackle play
to the weak side.

The ball is snapped to the tailback, who delays momentarily with the ball to allow the strong-side blockers to get to their weak-side positions. Then he runs the same pattern to the weak side as he would in the off-tackle play to the strong side. (See Figure 37.)

The fullback and blocking back team up on the defensive end. The weak-side end and tackle block the defensive tackle to the inside. The wingback and both guards lead the ball carrier through the hole.

Wedge play. Against an odd defense, the center is the apex of our wedge. Against an even defense, the strong-side guard is the apex.

If the center is the apex, he gives the fullback a very easy snap and then drives forward. The two guards drive in toward the center and forward so that the three of them are leading the wedge. The tackles and ends also drive in and forward to seal up the inside gaps. (See Figure 38.)

When the fullback has two yards or less to make for the first down or score, he dives over the line of scrimmage. The linemen must block low and hard so that he can get over them more easily. If he has more than two yards to make, he must stay on his feet and try to get daylight wherever he can find it.

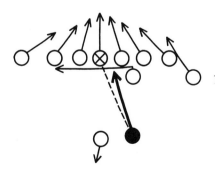

FIG. 38   Wedge play.

Area wedge play. Another excellent play to use when there are less than two yards to go for the first down or score is the area wedge play. The strong-side end leads the wedge, with the wingback and strong-side tackle blocking to the inside and the blocking back blocking to the outside.

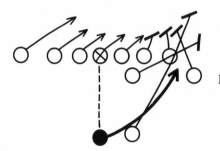

FIG. 39   Area Wedge play.

The tailback takes an easy snap from the center and follows the fullback toward the outside hip of the strong-side end, diving, if necessary, for the needed yardage.

The Buck-Lateral Series

Short trap. The fullback receives the snap from center and drives straight ahead, faking to the blocking back who has pivoted around to face him. (See Figure 40.)

The weak-side guard pulls and traps the first man through on the strong side of the center.

FIG. 40   Short trap.
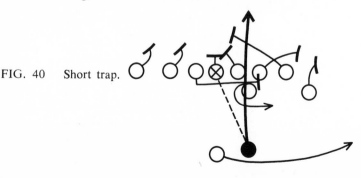

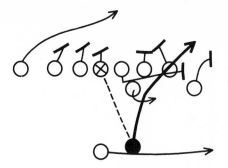

FIG. 41   Long trap.

Long trap. The fullback receives the snap and drives straight ahead, angling off to the right after faking to the blocking back. (See Figure 41.)

The strong-side guard pulls and traps out at the hole.

Buck-lateral off-tackle. The fullback receives the snap from center and drives straight ahead, handing the ball off to the blocking back who has pivoted around to face him. The blocking back carries the ball toward the strong-side end. (See Figure 42.) If the defensive end comes in, the blocking back pitches the ball back to the tailback. If the end plays wide, the blocking back keeps the ball and turns upfield.

Both guards pull. The strong-side guard blocks out on the defensive end. The weak-side guard helps run interference through the off-tackle hole. The wingback and strong-side end double-team the defensive tackle.

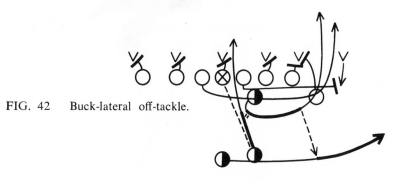

FIG. 42   Buck-lateral off-tackle.

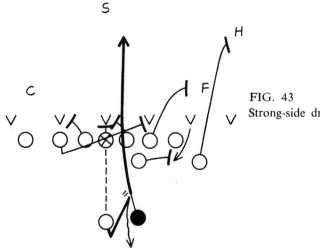

FIG. 43
Strong-side draw trap.

Draw Series

Strong-side draw trap. This particular draw play was designed to be run against a defense that has a man opposite the center and two "pinchers" on the inside shoulders of the tackles. (See Figure 43.)

As the tailback receives the snap from center, the fullback begins to drive straight ahead. Holding onto the ball with both hands, the tailback "rides" it in the fullback's belly. At the last moment the fullback takes the ball and the tailback drops back to fake the pass.

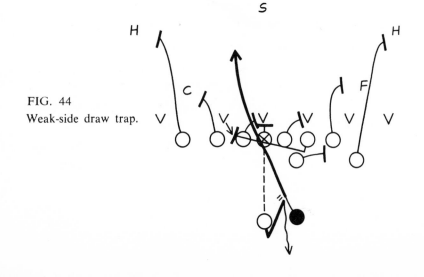

FIG. 44
Weak-side draw trap.

Weak-side draw trap. The backfield maneuvering in the weak-side draw trap is the same as in the previous play, except that the hole is on the weak side of center. (See Figure 44.) The fullback should stay as close to the two-on-one block of the center and weak-side guard as he can, since the trap out by the strong-side tackle is a difficult block to make.

Draw wedge play. The draw wedge combines the blocking of the straight series wedge plays and the backfield movements of the draw series. (See Figure 45.)

The blocking back blocks to the weak side and the wingback closes the gap to his inside.

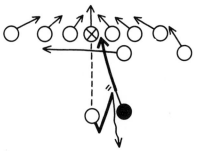

FIG. 45   Draw wedge play.

Draw reverse play. The tailback receives the snap from center and "rides" the ball in the fullback's belly as in the other draw plays. At the last moment the tailback pulls the ball back out and holds it in front of him, handing off to the wingback who is running toward the weak side. (See Figure 46.) The tailback then drops back to fake the pass. The fullback continues running into the line.

The blocking back and strong-side guard block the weak-side end. The wingback has the option of running outside the end or cutting in.

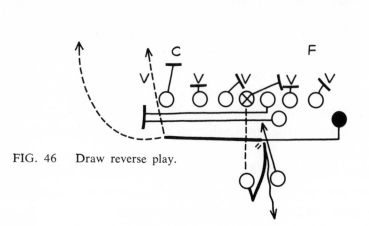

FIG. 46   Draw reverse play.

The Tailback-Spin Series

In the tailback-spin series, every play begins with the tailback receiving the snap from center and spinning. He may then hand off to the fullback, fake to the fullback and hand off to the wingback, or throw a running-pass.

If the fullback is the ball carrier, he may hit any hole between the weak-side guard and end. (See Figure 47.)

If the tailback fakes to the fullback and hands off to the wingback, the play goes around the weak-side end.

A third possibility, the tailback-spin running-pass, is described in detail on page 117.

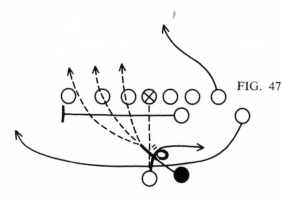

FIG. 47   Tailback-spin series.

Single Wingback Passes

Straight series running-pass option. The center snaps the ball to the tailback with a slight lead to the strong side. The tailback fakes toward the line of scrimmage to keep the strong-side defensive end from penetrating too deep in the backfield. Then the tailback runs toward the sideline.

The fullback and blocking back drive shoulder-to-shoulder at the strong-side defensive end, but at the last moment the blocking back slides along the line of scrimmage for the pass.

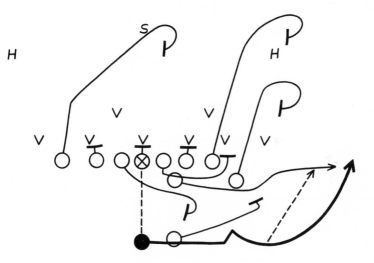

FIG. 48   Straight series running-pass option.

If the defensive end is blocked well by the fullback, the tailback can run the ball. If the end is not blocked well, the tailback will throw the ball.

Straight series running-pass option to the weak side. If the defense is over-shifted to our strong side, the running-pass option can be run to the weak side very effectively. (See

Figure 49.) The backfield assignments are the same as in the running-pass option to the strong side.

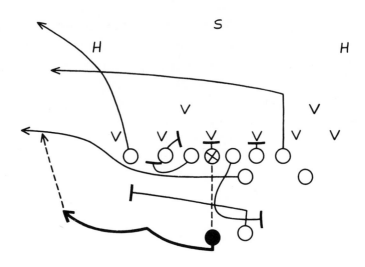

FIG. 49   Straight series running-pass option to the weak side.

Buck-lateral running-pass. The fullback receives the snap and drives straight ahead, handing off the ball to the blocking back who has pivoted around to face him. The blocking back then runs toward the strong-side sideline, pitching the ball back to the tailback, who immediately hits the wing-back with the pass. (See Figure 50.)

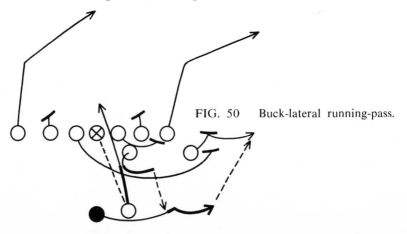

FIG. 50   Buck-lateral running-pass.

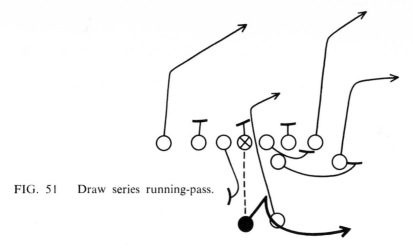

FIG. 51   Draw series running-pass.

Draw series running-pass. The tailback receives the snap from center and "rides" the ball in the fullback's belly as in the other draw plays. At the last moment the tailback pulls the ball out and runs back and to the strong side as quickly as possible. (See Figure 51.)

The wingback and both ends are potential receivers.

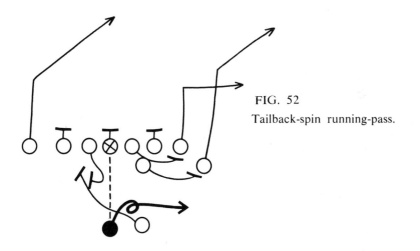

FIG. 52
Tailback-spin running-pass.

Tailback-spin running-pass. The tailback receives the snap from center, spins, fakes to the fullback, and runs to the strong side, throwing to one of the ends or the wingback. (See Figure 52.)

The fullback blocks the weak-side end. The blocking back blocks the strong-side end.

Single Wingback Quick Kick

In the single wing quick kick, the tailback takes three quick steps (right-left-right, for the right-footed kicker) to the rear just before the ball is snapped. As soon as the kick is away, the tailback covers to the weak side.

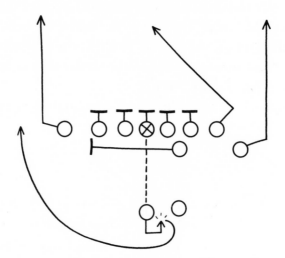

FIG. 53   Single wingback quick kick.

The blocking back blocks the first man outside the weak-side tackle and then covers to the weak side. The fullback blocks the first man outside the strong-side tackle and then covers to the strong side. (See Figure 53.)

The wingback and weak-side end are the contain men, covering the kick to the outside. The strong-side end goes for the ball immediately.

CHAPTER EIGHT

Secrets of the Split T

DON FAUROT
University of Missouri

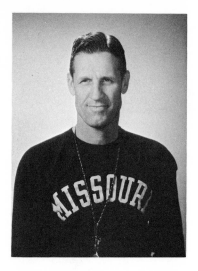

DON FAUROT, recently elected to Football's Hall of Fame, has been associated with the University of Missouri as a player, coach, and athletic director for more than 40 years.

As an undergraduate at Missouri, Faurot lettered in football, basketball, and baseball. Then from 1935 through 1956 (with three years out for war service), he coached the Missouri grid teams, posting an enviable 101-79-10 record and producing four all-Americans, including Hall of Fame member "Pitchin' Paul" Christman. During his 28 total years of active coaching, Faurot's grid teams compiled an overall 164-92-13 record.

In 1941 Faurot introduced his famous Split T formation at Missouri, winning conference titles in 1941 and 1942, and catapulting the Tigers into football's big-time. During World War II, Faurot popularized the Split T when he coached the Iowa Navy Pre-flight team, losing only to Notre Dame in 1943 and the Jacksonville Fliers in 1944.

A past-president of the American Football Coaches Association, Faurot has authored a popular coaching book, *Football: Secrets of the Split T Formation.* (Prentice-Hall, Inc., Englewood Cliffs, N. J., 1950.)

Secrets of the Split T

The Split T formation with its wider line spacing and its sliding quarterback was conceived at the University of Missouri in 1941. It all began after we had graduated our ace passer, Paul Christman, who later quarterbacked so ably for the Chicago Cardinals. Christman had fit nicely into our Single Wing and Short Punt formations, and his passing arm had carried us to a conference championship and an Orange Bowl appearance.

His departure meant the loss of a fine tailback, and there was no suitable tailback replacement in sight among the returning lettermen. However, our veteran backs had considerable speed, and the squad as a whole was versatile. The time seemed ripe for innovating the basic plays of the Split T, and this we did tentatively in spring practice, at the same time retaining some of our Single Wing offense.

The 1941 Missouri team pioneered the way of the Split T in superb style. They led the nation in net rushing per game with an average of 307 yards. This team finished sixth in total offense, won the then Big Six championship and earned a Sugar Bowl bid. In 1942, the Missouri team was fifth in rushing offense and again won the conference championship. In 1943 a shift of scene took me to Iowa City, Iowa, where my Iowa Navy Pre-flight team used the Split T exclusively to set a new rushing record of 324.4 yards per game (a record since broken several times, however). The total offense was second best in the nation that year, indicating that the system could launch an effective passing attack.

The Split T had passed its trial test successfully by the time of my return to Missouri in 1946. In 1947, the final statistics showed Missouri sixth in rushing offense and eighth in total offense. The 1948 team placed seventh in rushing offense and tenth in total offense. In 1949, Missouri's total offense ranked eighth in the national picture, and passing had become an integral part of the offense.

We cite these figures merely to underscore the fact that the Split T has paid dividends at Missouri. It should be stressed here that these results, save for the year at Iowa Pre-flight, were realized with average personnel—athletes of ordinary size and talents. Our year-in, year-out players were just that, although there were always welcome exceptions.

Those of us who have grown up with the Split T have acquired certain convictions about its offensive value. The four basic reasons for our preferring this system are:

1. It requires only average personnel.
2. It averages more yards per play.
3. It springs the backs into the open field more often.
4. It puts greater pressure on standard defenses.

Personnel

Any coach would have a made-to-order team if 50 per cent of his backfield material consisted of well-knit 195-pounders—big, fast, and shifty—and if half of his aspiring linemen were rugged, rangy, and possessed of a love of contact. He would have a corner on championships if these same able-bodied athletes had native ability, intelligence and competitive fire to accompany their physical qualifications. Unfortunately, it doesn't work out that way. As a general rule, if the average football player has size, then he lacks speed and agility. If he has speed and reacts well, then he often needs stature and weight. Or he may measure up to the physical standards but be slow to learn or too easygoing to fire up.

Darold Jenkins, all-American center on Coach Faurot's first split T team at Missouri.

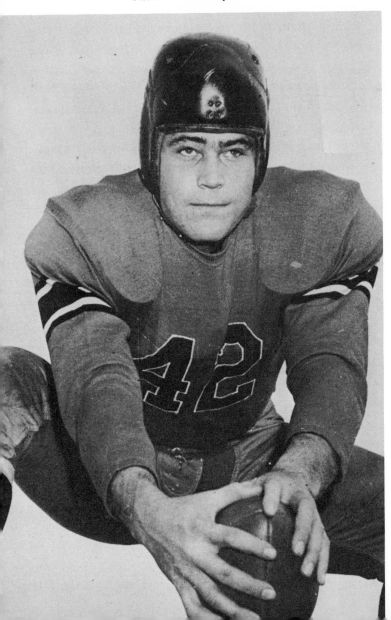

The "dream" player who has what it takes in every department is as rare as a ruby and is coveted just as much. Rival coaches respect no state boundary lines when such a boy may be obtained, but like the biggest trout in the stream, he often gets away.

Therefore, remembering that most football players are ordinary boys of ordinary talents, we must examine what we consider the first and most significant reason for preferring the Split T offense: *It requires only average personnel.*

Successful use of the Split T is not contingent upon having an excellent passer. Neither does it depend on having exceptional break-away runners. Although the line need not be big and fast, it must be reasonably active if the system is to function properly. We do not mean that the great passer, runner, or lineman has no place in the Split T, but emphasize only that this system can be successful without individual headliners.

In the Split T aerial game, any one of three backs does the tossing. The quarterback need not be a sharp passer, but he must be able to connect on some of the shorter pass plays. The pitch-outs or running passes provide a strong auxiliary weapon. Their deceptiveness helps to set up easier blocking for the halfback who may elect to turn downfield with the ball if his receivers do not get clear. These pass plays often develop into end runs that make substantial gains.

The Split T does not require the triple-threat back who can run, pass or punt such as some other formations need. Bob Steuber, Missouri's all-American halfback in 1942, was as gifted a climax runner as it has been my privilege to coach. Steuber was not, however, a triple-threater, and none of the backs who followed him were as talented. Yet, the Missouri team's rushing offense as well as total offense, ranked consistently among the nation's top ten.

Bob Steuber, all-American halfback at Missouri.

In the line, too, the essentials of one-on-one blocking can be taught easily. Because of the wider line spacing, the lineman need not overpower his opponent to "make the hole." It already exists; he must merely maintain it. Fast, mobile guards, so necessary in some formations, are not a must in the Split T because the blockers preceding the play generally move straight downfield instead of pulling out to lead the ball-carrier.

The tackles, usually the biggest men on a squad, are matched with the defensive tackles. This saves wear and tear on the smaller ends because they are not required to mix with opposing tackles on virtually every play.

Although the University of Missouri team had no exceptional personnel in 1949, the Split T offense enabled us to lead the nation in the number of first downs made during our ten-game season. According to the National Collegiate Bureau of Statistics, we gained the "first and ten" 181 times, enough to out rank all other college teams in this department. This should prove that the Split T is a sound possession-of-the-ball offense.

Average Yardage Per Play

When both the Split T and Single Wing offenses were used at Missouri, we discovered two things as the season progressed. First, our quarterback was using more Split T plays because the team seemed to prefer them. Second, statistics proved that the Split T plays were outgaining the Single Wing plays almost two to one. Since the same personnel were running both Single Wing and Split T plays against the same defenses and opponents, we had a valid comparison. To us, the evidence was conclusive.

Springs Back Into Open

We found that the Split T springs the backs into the open more frequently than our previous offensive systems. When using both systems, our backs made more long gains from the Split T plays than they could from our Single Wing plays. The handoff play hit a split second faster than any play from any other offense, and the interference was able to get down field ahead of the runner more easily. Our pitch-out end runs were more difficult for the defensive ends to handle, enabling our backs to make long gains more frequently.

The statistics also showed that our backs were scoring many touchdowns from 20 yards or more out in the field. We believe that this was a result of the greater deception inherent in the offense. The ability to get our backs into the open made possible the use of smaller, more elusive half-backs, who were numerous on our squad. They did not have to depend on their weight and drive in order to break clear.

Pressure On Standard Defenses

Our experience in using and in playing against the Split T has convinced us that this offense is much harder to stop with a standard defense than any other offensive system. The Split T has been very successful against the basic five-, six-, or seven-man lines with a three-deep secondary.

The splits in the line open defensive holes wider, thus affording better blocking angles for the offensive linemen. The split line also permits the one-on-one blocking which is necessary in order to get a number of the other interference men ahead of the play. The blocks need not be sustained as long, nor must the defensive man be moved as far, since he is more or less screened out of the play with a high block. If the defense refuses to open up when the offense splits its formation, outside blocking angles are easily gained, and wide plays have increased chances of success.

Many of our opponents have brought up nine men to within one yard of the line of scrimmage in an effort to stop the running game of the Split T. Simple arithmetic shows, however, that this weakens their pass defense. In order to move the ball against these very tight box defenses, the team must be able to pass. Flanker backs are also necessary to loosen up these compact nine-man fronts.

Although the slanting and looping lines have been fairly effective in stopping the Split T plays, the linebackers are generally used as linemen, again weakening the defense just over the line against quick or hook passes. This unorthodox slanting defense is a guessing game and the guessers are apt to come up with the wrong answer if zone blocking rules are developed.

The best reason we can advance for continuing to use the Split T is the success it has given us in running against standard eight-man fronts. In these defenses, only eight men are within two yards of the line of scrimmage. The defense may be placed in 4-4-2-1, 5-3-2-1, 6-2-2-1, or 7-1-2-1 alignments. If the opponents use a nine-man front, namely, the 5-4-2, the 6-3-2 or the 7-2-2, the deceptiveness of the Split T will hold the linebackers in tight enough to enable our pass receivers to shake open with regularity. If our passers can connect with their targets, then we can move the ball through the air.

MECHANICS OF THE SPLIT T

The Split T formation got its name from the split of the line. Splitting the line in offensive football means leaving a space between the linemen, providing them with a definite blocking advantage. The following diagrams show the standard split against the five-, six-, and seven-man lines.

Split against five-man line. Against the five-man defensive alignment shown in Figure 54, our tackles split the full 36

FIG. 54

Split against five-man line.

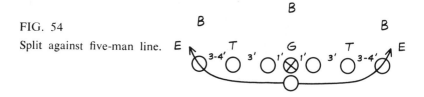

inches in order to gain a head-on position with defensive tackles. Our tackle closes the split only when the defensive tackle lines up to his inside. As long as our tackle is head on, he is expected to prevent the defensive tackle from crashing inside and getting to the exchange point of the ball ahead of our offensive backs. This split away from the center of our guards and tackles places the defensive man that much wider, thus providing us with a larger hole inside the defensive tackle through which to move. If the defensive tackle does not spread to meet our offensive tackle, we have an excellent outside blocking position on him. This helps our wide attack.

Our offensive end has a working distance of one to two yards against a standard five-man line, but he may widen still more in order to keep the defensive end from crashing too hard and from getting to the exchange point of the basic Split T plays.

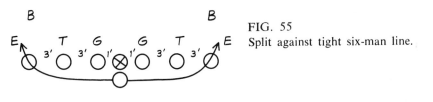

FIG. 55
Split against tight six-man line.

Split against tight six-man line. The split in Figure 55 is almost the same for the tackles as that on the five-man line. This is approximately three feet, but it may be widened slightly to enable our offensive tackle to gain blocking position for both inside and outside plays. Our offensive end may play two to six feet from his offensive tackle. Our guards again have a working distance of approximately one to two feet. This split keeps the defensive guards on a six-man line from playing to the outside of our guards. The blocking on wide plays is thus facilitated for the offensive guards. If the defensive guards play too wide, there is an unusually large hole up the middle for the quarterback sneak, the fastest hitting play in football. This is almost an automatic call by our quarterback when the defensive guards play wide.

Split against wide six-man line. The wide six-man line as shown in Figure 56 does not demand as wide a split of the offensive tackles and end as does that against the tight six-man line. When the defensive tackle wishes to play head on with our offensive end, the split should be closed to two feet for both the tackle and the end. The split of the guards would be the same as that shown in Figure 55. If line-backers move into the line to form an eight-man line, the offensive tackle and end should split off six inches wider. The four-man line may have an alignment identical to that in Figure 56.

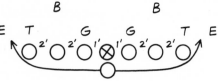

FIG. 56
Split against wide six-man line.

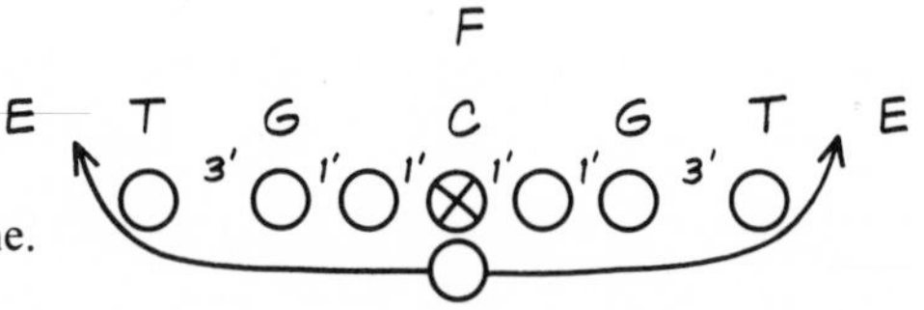

FIG. 57
Split against seven-man line.

Split against seven-man line. The seven-man line shown in Figure 57 presents a different problem for the offensive line. The offensive tackle closes to one foot, the same split taken by the offensive guard. The offensive end moves to three or four feet in an effort to keep a fairly wide defensive hole inside the tackle. If the defensive tackle fails to move out with the end, our end has flanking position for wide plays. The one rule that must be taught to the split offensive line is that it is imperative to tighten up when the defensive men who are to be blocked move inside. They will attempt to shoot the gap or to crash between the split in the line. The offensive lineman must be ready to block to the inside when this occurs.

Path of Quarterback

The Split T quarterback operates up and down the line parallel to the line of scrimmage, as shown in Figures 54, 55, 56, and 57. Since he should never be more than one yard back of the line, the Split T permits a faster-hitting handoff play than the other T formations.

The running pitch-out end run is executed by the quarterback from this path, thus keeping the exchange of the ball so close to the line that the defensive players do not have time to diagnose more than one of the basic plays, increasing the deceptiveness of the offense. The teaching of this system must include intensive work with the quarterbacks to keep them moving along the correct path.

If the quarterback is moving right, he should take a one-foot step with his right foot in his direction of travel as the ball is snapped to him. On his second step he can either reach the handoff man hitting into the line or fake to him and continue on his designated path to set up one of the other players.

One of the most common faults of coaches who try to run the Split T is allowing the quarterback to move too deep in the backfield when running the basic plays. It cannot be emphasized too often that the quarterback must follow the straight and narrow path if this offense is to be successful. Much time should be spent in confronting him with all the hazards that might appear on this course so that he will know how to cope with them if they occur under game conditions.

Center and Quarterback Exchange

A critical need in any T formation offense is a smooth exchange between the center and the quarterback. In the Split T offense the quarterback must move laterally as fast as possible in full possession of the ball with his body under control. The center must hold the ball as far in front of himself as he can comfortably extend it. The offensive guards and tackles should also move up to the ball to take their feet out of the way of the quarterback. If the center places the ball too closely under his head, the guards must move their feet back of the center's feet, thereby penning up the quarterback.

The center should be a fairly large individual who can withstand the jolts of a hard-charging defensive lineman and not let them interfere with his pass to the quarterback. His head and eyes should be up and on the defense. Although he passes blind to the quarterback, he should be able to feel the quarterback's hands in position to receive the snapped ball.

The quarterback. The heels and thumbs of the quarterback's hands should be held together tightly as he takes the ball from the center. His elbows must be flexed to absorb the jar of a hard pass; his fingers should be relaxed and pointing straight downward. He stands erect but flat-footed with knees slightly bent, feet even but well apart, and with most of his weight on the balls of his feet. From this position he can move rapidly to the right or to the left.

The exchange. The center should snap the ball firmly in one continuous movement so that the exchange is executed quickly. The quarterback should then follow the center with a pushing movement of both hands as the center charges ahead for his block. This pressure on the center helps to prevent fumbles during the exchange and permits him to be a full blocking lineman. This is important when a good man is playing opposite the center.

The ball is exchanged higher than in most T systems. We feel that this is basic to the fast getaway on the quarterback's path down the line. There is a limit to the speed at which the quarterback can move laterally from his position back of the center, but with constant practice he can learn to be in motion as he takes the ball and still operate with a minimum number of miscues.

Sequence of Plays

The Split T offense affords one of the finest sequences of plays in football. There are four of the basic plays in each direction, on all of which the quarterback and the other members of the backfield start with the same steps in the same direction and in exactly the same manner.

Figure 58 shows the path of the backs on these four plays moving to the right:

1. The handoff to the right halfback.
2. The quarterback keep.
3. The running pitch-out to the left halfback.
4. The running pass by the left halfback.

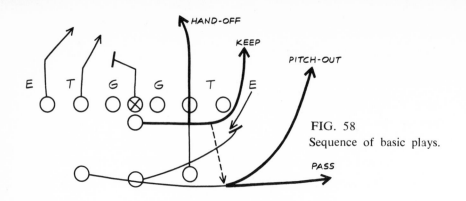

FIG. 58
Sequence of basic plays.

The quarterback may hand off to the right halfback hitting in, a play second only to the quarterback sneak in hitting speed; he may continue on down the line of scrimmage and turn off-tackle for the fast developing play known as the quarterback keep; or he may lateral the ball on the run—called the running pitch-out. This pitch-out enables the left halfback to run around the end, using the fullback as a blocker. The running pass develops in the same manner as the pitch-out, and the ball-handling is the same.

All of these plays are used both right and left, and all the backs keep to a given course regardless of which one carries the ball. The manner in which the ball moves, not the path of the players, determines the play to be used. Initiating all four of these basic plays in the same manner puts tremendous pressure on the defensive tackle and the defensive end.

Since the linemen generally block the same opponent on each play, taking him in or out according to the assignment, the blocking of the line in this basic sequence of plays changes very little. On the pass play, however, the blocking is slightly different because the end is always sent down as a receiver. There are actually very few tip-offs to help a linebacker or a defensive lineman diagnose the coming play.

The Fullback Belly Series with one flanked halfback is a necessary addition to the four basic Split T plays.

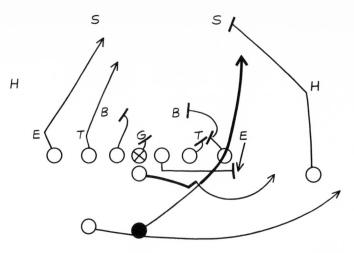

FIG. 59   Fullback slant play with halfback flanker.

The fullback slant play provides a hard-hitting smash from which the wide belly option play may be called. On the fullback slant, a cross block may be used with the guard blocking out at the hole and the tackle and end blocking in on opposing linemen or linebackers. (See Figure 59.)

When the belly option play is called, the quarterback rides with the fullback for a good fake and then continues on for a wide option play where he may fake and keep the ball or may pitch out to the halfback coming around. (See Figure 60.) The guard moves out and blocks the opposing end in so the play may go wide.

FIG. 60   Outside belly option play with halfback flanker.

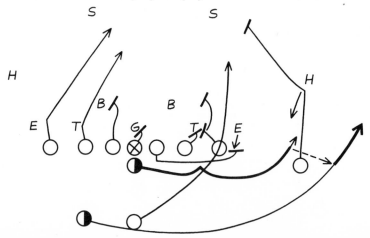

The quarterback belly pass also should be included in this series. (See Figure 61.) When the quarterback throws from the belly series, the left halfback blocks the end on the right, allowing three receivers to go out.

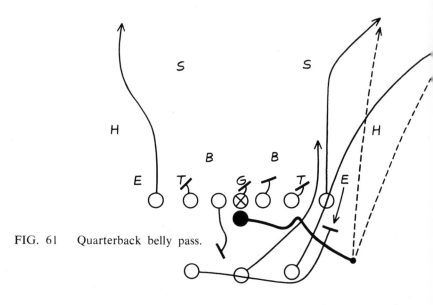

FIG. 61   Quarterback belly pass.

On the goal line, the fullback slant play may be executed from the standing "T" with a solid blocking line and the halfback blocking the end out. (See Figure 62.) This is one of football's best plays for a yard or on the goal line where the defense becomes very tight and tough.

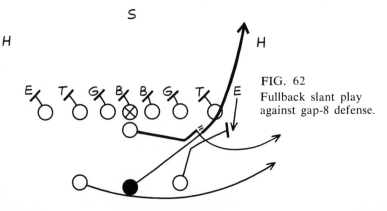

FIG. 62
Fullback slant play
against gap-8 defense.

Backfield Stance

When operating the Split T offense, the backs must be able to move rapidly when the charge signal is called. Their stance is therefore very important. We firmly believe that it is necessary to put the backs down on a three-point stance in order to avoid backfield-in-motion penalties. In this position the backs are more stable and need not lean in order to get a satisfactory start. The halfback's stance is similar, with two exceptions, to that of a 100-yard dash man. The stagger and spacing of the feet are almost the same as those for a sprinter's start except that the halfback's feet are a little farther apart. The halfback places one hand down instead of two and uses the elbow of the other arm against his thigh for a pushoff in the direction he wishes to go.

Halfback's Stance. The right halfback should assume a stance with his inside (left) foot back. He must be able to move quickly in only two directions: to his left for the wide plays, and straight ahead for the fast-hitting handoff plays. The reverse is true of the left halfback: he places his inside (right) foot back for a fast start straight ahead or to his right. Our experimentation with stance and its bearing on quick starts has convinced us that the stance described above has the best results for halfbacks. We have had few backfield-in-motion penalties.

If our halfbacks go out as flankers, they can use the stance required by their position and still get away fast for passes and for downfield blocks.

Fullback's Stance. The fullback uses an entirely different stance since he must be able to start to his right or to his left with equal speed. His is a three-point stance with feet wide apart, affording fast lateral movement without first being in motion. It also permits a fairly fast start straight ahead, and will not handicap the quick step or fake used in fullback counter plays.

Backfield Position

Figure 63 shows the approximate position of the backs in the Split T formation. The halfbacks are usually four yards and the fullback four and a half yards from the line of scrimmage. There are two yards between the halfbacks and the fullbacks. This is a wider backfield than in most formations, but it is necessary because of the split line which makes the defensive holes wider.

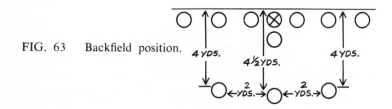

FIG. 63   Backfield position.

Ball-Handling

The quarterback carries the ball in two hands and, while in motion, he laterals with a two-hand, underhand pass. The running pitch-out is one of the best plays in the series. In this play, the ball is thrown while the quarterback moves rapidly down the line on a path just inside the defensive end.

On the handoff plays the ball is placed directly in front of the halfback who is hitting in for the handoff play, and the halfback can look straight ahead to focus his attention on the hole he is heading for. The quarterback is responsible for placing the ball in the correct spot—on the halfback's far hip. He must do this with one hand, and his wrist should be limp. In taking the ball, the halfback raises his near elbow and forearm while holding his far hand just hip high. The far hand acts as a stop to prevent the ball from going all the way through. The top arm and hand are lowered after the ball is placed on his hip. The lower hand actually contacts the ball first. The raised forearm acts as a guard or protection against any defensive player who might meet the play at the point of exchange. It will help the halfback to keep possession of the ball. When faking a handoff, the halfback hitting in uses a motion identical to that used when taking the ball. The quarterback fakes the ball to him with two hands and then continues on his way.

Good faking by the quarterback and the other offensive backs enhances the deceptiveness of this sequence of plays. When not receiving the ball, the halfbacks should carry out their fakes to a point five yards across the line of scrimmage. When the quarterback is running the keep play off-tackle, he not only fakes to the handoff man hitting in but also makes a two-handed fake to the pitch-out man coming around.

The lateral or pitch-out pass should be made with a dead ball that is thrown without English or any turning motion. This type of pass hangs in the air and is much easier for the halfbacks to catch on the run. It is always thrown with two hands.

Learning Assignments

One of the secrets of any successful offense is simplification of the players' offensive assignments. We try to have very few offensive plays, but those must be made adaptable to all the defenses that may confront us. We classify defenses in three categories: *The even defenses, the odd defenses,* and *the slanting and looping defenses.*

The even defenses. In each of these defenses the guards are opposite the offensive guards. The offensive center is free to move ahead for blocking assignments downfield.

1. Four-man line, which is a 4-4-2-1.
2. Six-man line, which is a 6-2-2-1.
3. Eight-man line, which is an 8-3.

The odd defenses. Each of these defenses has a player opposite our center. The guards are usually free to go through for the secondary.

1. Five-man line, which is a 5-3-2-1.
2. Seven-man line, which is a 7-1-2-1.
3. Over-shifted six right, which is a 6-2-2-1.
4. Over-shifted left, which is a 6-2-2-1.
5. Nine-man line, which is a 9-2.

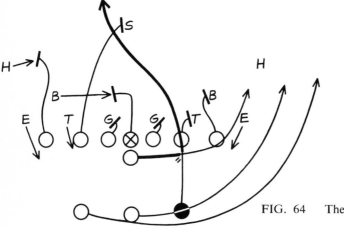

FIG. 64   The straight handoff.

We learn all plays in two ways: *against the odd defenses,* and *against the even defenses.* Most of our primary blocking assignments call for each offensive lineman to block the man who lines up in front of him. When there is no defensive man in front of the lineman, he goes through for the linebackers or deep secondary.

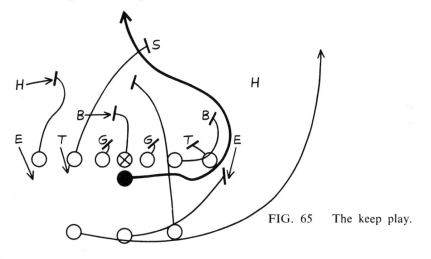

FIG. 65   The keep play.

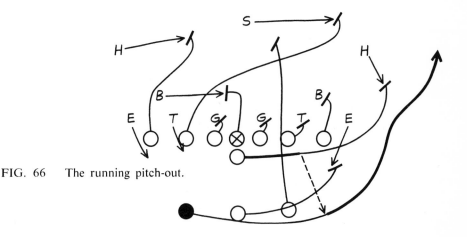

FIG. 66   The running pitch-out.

Slanting and looping lines. It is very difficult to teach exact assignments in the slanting and looping defenses, but we try to impress two cardinal principles upon our linemen and our backs. First, the offensive linemen must take the defensive linemen according to the way the latter start to go in their loop. Second, our backs must hit directly over the original positions of the defensive linemen because the defenders will move to the right or left in the slanting or looping.

Our offensive linemen relay to our quarterback the information about the defensive line's method of play. They should keep him informed when our opponents seem to be using unorthodox defenses by slanting and looping in an effort to stop our ground attack. Considerable practice time must be devoted to preparing to meet this type of defense if players are to feel at home when they encounter it.

If we are thoroughly familiar with our few offensive plays against the odd and even defenses and if we have some principles for working against the slanting and looping defenses, we then have a good chance of keeping our offense rolling and of making substantial progress down the field with the ball.

Position Requirements

Although exceptional players are not necessary for a satisfactory offense with the Split T, there are certain fundamental requirements for the backfield personnel.

Quarterback. The quarterback should be a heady ball-handler and preferably a player who has had some basketball experience. He should be able to pass and run well with the ball.

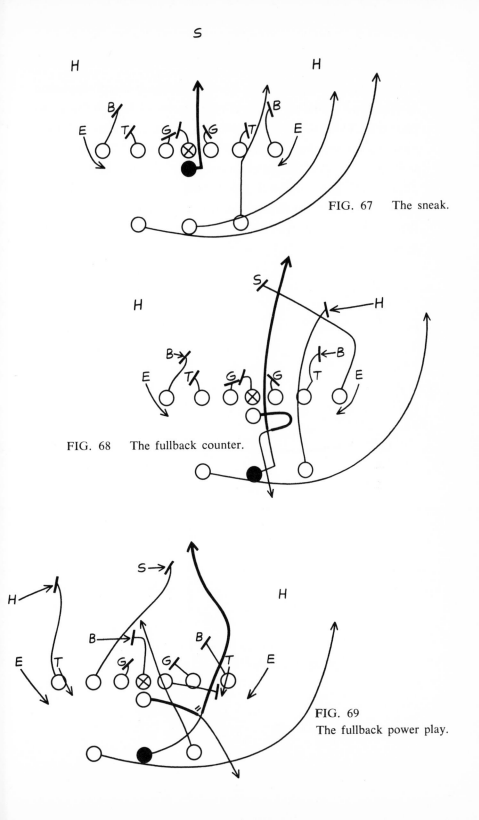

FIG. 67   The sneak.

FIG. 68   The fullback counter.

FIG. 69
The fullback power play.

In the Split T at Missouri our quarterback was always one of the team's leading ground gainers by virtue of the keep play off-tackle, a play used often against goal line defenses or when a yard was needed for a first down. Although passing ability is not absolutely necessary for the quarterback, almost any player can learn to throw the hook, sideline, jump, or buck pass. When we had a quarterback who could throw, the roll out and Belly Series passes were always our most effective.

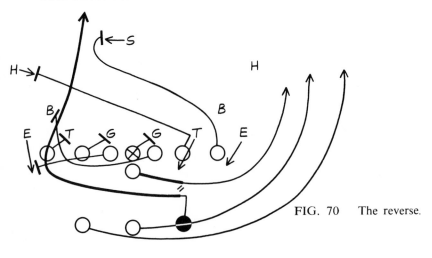

FIG. 70   The reverse.

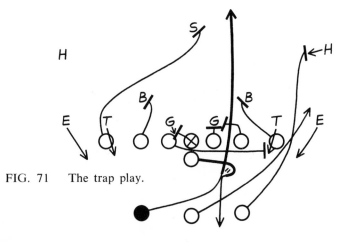

FIG. 71   The trap play.

Fullback. The fullback in the Split T must be a good blocker, like the blocking back in the Single Wing system. He is the work horse of the offense. His ability to carry the ball is also important because of the Belly Series plays.

Halfbacks. The halfbacks, usually the fastest men in the Split T backfield, should be good runners in the open field, and should also be able to throw a running pass. There are two reasons for our preferring the running pass. First, we believe that halfbacks learn to throw the running pass more easily than they do the standing pass, and second, if his receivers do not open up, it is much simpler for the halfback to hold the ball and, with his momentum already up, to turn downfield.

Although the above requirements do not seem overly exacting, exceptional ability is welcomed in any of the backfield spots. Strong running ability may be featured in any of the four backfield positions. It is also possible for all four of the backfield men to throw if they have the ability to do so.

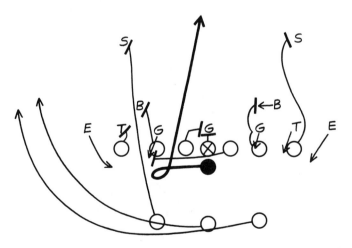

FIG. 72   Oklahoma's quarterback spinner play.

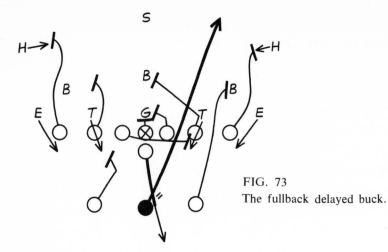

S

FIG. 73
The fullback delayed buck.

FIG. 74   The Statue of Liberty play.

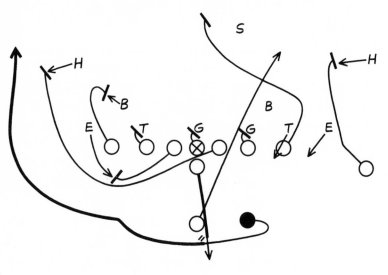

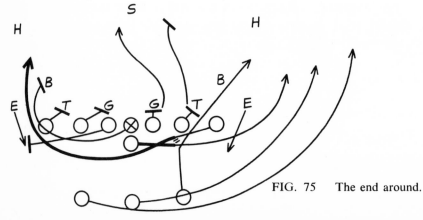

FIG. 75   The end around.

Flexibility

The term "flexibility" is applied to a resourceful offense, one capable of adjusting quickly to any changes made in the defense while the play is under way. For example, if the defensive tackle crashes to his inside on the handoff play, the ball-carrier hitting in alertly can slide to the outside for a substantial gain even though the play was called inside.

If the pitch-out is called and the end floats or comes too far across the line of scrimmage, the quarterback may exercise the option of keeping the ball and running off-tackle, since the blocking is the same for the keep and the pitch-out plays.

If the defensive end smashes, the pitch-out can be made more quickly and the fullback who might be assigned to block the end can pass him up to take a linebacker or defensive halfback instead. The running passes may also develop into excellent fake pass and run plays when the secondary retreats quickly to cover the ends going deep. A modern offense must be flexible enough to adjust easily to the changing defenses.

As we sum up the "secrets" of the Split T, we see that though there seem to be many "secrets," they are, in reality, comparatively simple and easily taught. A long learning period is not required. In fact, many teams that have taken up the Split T have had successful seasons their first year.

Split T Plays

Figures 64—75 illustrate several of the basic Split T plays. These plays are shown on pages 140-146.

CHAPTER NINE

The Delaware Winged T

Dave Nelson
University of Delaware

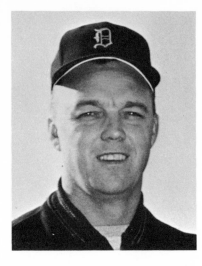

DAVE NELSON, head football coach at the University of Delaware since 1951, is the most successful coach in the school's 70-year gridiron history. "The Admiral" holds a 60-31-2 record at Delaware and an overall log of 81-37-6 in his 15 years as a head coach.

During his undergraduate days at the University of Michigan, Nelson himself was an outstanding football player. A teammate of the famed Tom Harmon, Nelson led the Wolverine squad in rushing during his senior year with an average of 6.31 yards per carry. Upon graduation he was awarded the Big Ten medal for combined excellence in scholastic achievement and athletics.

Nelson, a brilliant strategist, is probably best known for developing and nurturing the Winged T into national acceptance. He and his former teammate and longtime friend, Forest Evashevski, brought the Winged T into prominence during the late 1950's through the outstanding records of their teams at Delaware and Iowa, and through their popular coaching book, *Scoring Power from the Winged T*. (The Wm. C. Brown Co., Dubuque, Ia., 1957). Nelson has since authored another highly regarded book, *Football—Principles and Play*. (The Ronald Press Company, New York, N. Y., 1962.)

The Delaware Winged T

Although our Winged T had its start at the University of Maine in 1950, it didn't reach fulfillment until the next year when we moved it to the University of Delaware. At Maine we did not have an outstanding tailback or center for our Single Wing attack, so a last minute switch was made to the T formation, but with the Single Wing blocking in the line retained. Midway through the season we began using a wing in the backfield and found that this provided us with a flexible, balanced offense with some of the best traits of both the T formation and the Single Wing.

At that time, most teams were running Split T and belly offenses with one-on-one blocking and a flow of backs in the direction of the play. When we began running counter plays from the Winged T at Delaware in 1951, the offense began to "click," despite the fact that the team did not block or execute it very well. Also, all of the teams that had been used to one-on-one blocking were not prepared at that time for the double-team blocks that we were using. With these two big advantages in our favor, we merely had to polish the offense and begin adding to it.

It was Iowa's success with the Winged T from 1956 to 1960 that brought the formation to popularity and widespread use. Forest Evashevski's Hawkeye teams won three Big Ten titles and two Rose Bowls within a five-year period, missing a fourth championship by a total of five points. Prior to that time, Iowa had not won a conference title in 34 years.

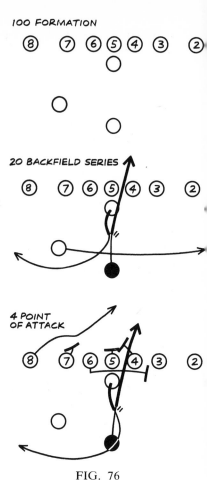

100 FORMATION

20 BACKFIELD SERIES

4 POINT OF ATTACK

Don Miller, one of Coach Nelson's great Winged T quarterbacks at Delaware.

FIG. 76

The Delaware Winged T can be credited with some Winged T innovations, but the use of wings in football is not a new idea at all. Frank Kavanaugh ran what he called a Winged T at Dartmouth in 1919. Lou Little and Tad Wieman used one with an unbalanced line at Columbia in 1945. Aldo "Buff" Donelli, Ray Elliot and "Rip" Engle all had great success with variations of the Winged T during the 40's. The Winged T, like so many other phases of football, has evolved over a period of many years, following a cycle of becoming more popular, fading out, and then becoming popular again with certain basic improvements.

NUMBERING SYSTEM*

The signal system employed in this Winged T offense consists of a play number of three digits. The first number indicates the formation, the second number the backfield series and techniques, and the third number indicates the point of attack. An example of this three digit system is play 124. (See Figure 76.)

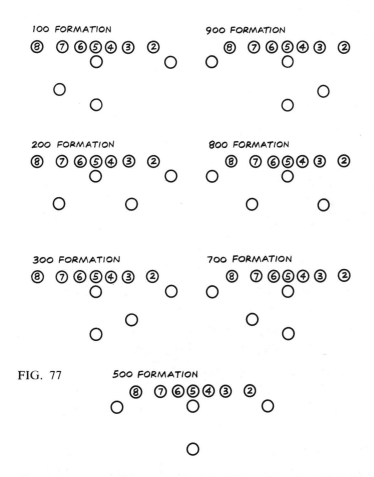

FIG. 77

* David M. Nelson and Forest Evashevski, *The Modern Winged T Play Book* (Dubuque, Iowa: Wm. C. Brown Company Publishers, 1961), pp. 3-9.

Formations

There are seven basic formations used in this system and these are always described in the first number of the three digit numbering system. (See Figure 77.) At Delaware, we use the 300 and 700 formations very sparingly.

Backfield Series

The second number indicates whether the play will be a run or a pass pattern play and the techniques of the backs. This digit uses nine numbers and all are series of running plays except 60 and 70. The 60 and 70 series are backfield techniques from which the quarterback passes the ball, and the line and backs block pass protection while the ends and the other backs run the pattern.

Mark Hurm, one of Delaware's outstanding centers.

9—⑧ ⑦ ⑥⑤④ ③ ②—¹ FIG. 78

Point of Attack

The third and last digit is the point of attack or the hole to be hit. There are nine points of attack numbered from right to left. With the exception of the two flank areas, the holes are numbered over the seven offensive linemen. (See Figure 78.)

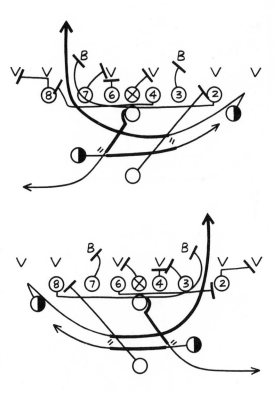

FIG. 79

WINGED T PLAYS

Each of the following plays may be diagrammed and run to the opposite side by mirroring the play. For example, the 138 counter criss cross becomes the 932 counter criss cross when it is mirrored. (See Figure 79.) Other plays are shown on pages 156-165.

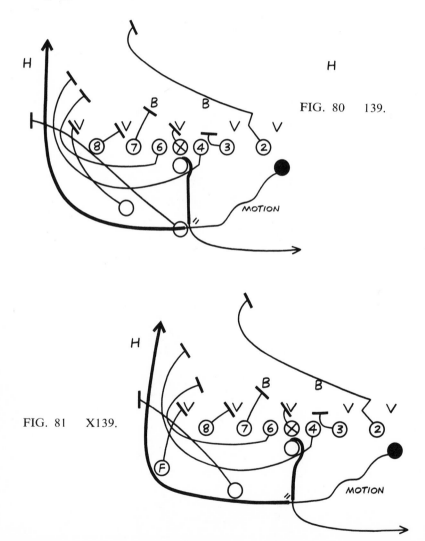

FIG. 80　139.

FIG. 81　X139.

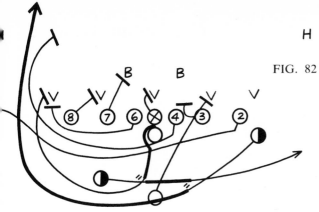

H

FIG. 82   139 counter criss cross.

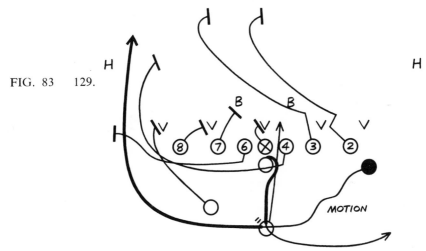

FIG. 83   129.

H   H

MOTION

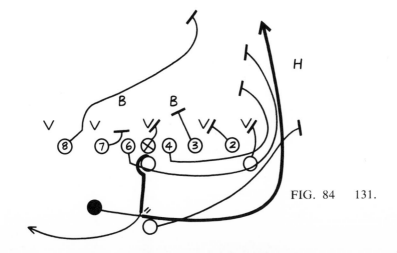

H   H

FIG. 84   131.

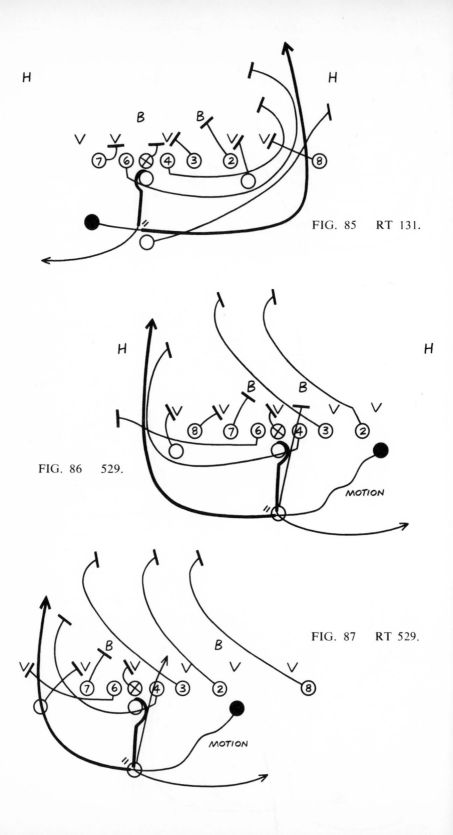

FIG. 85   RT 131.

FIG. 86   529.

FIG. 87   RT 529.

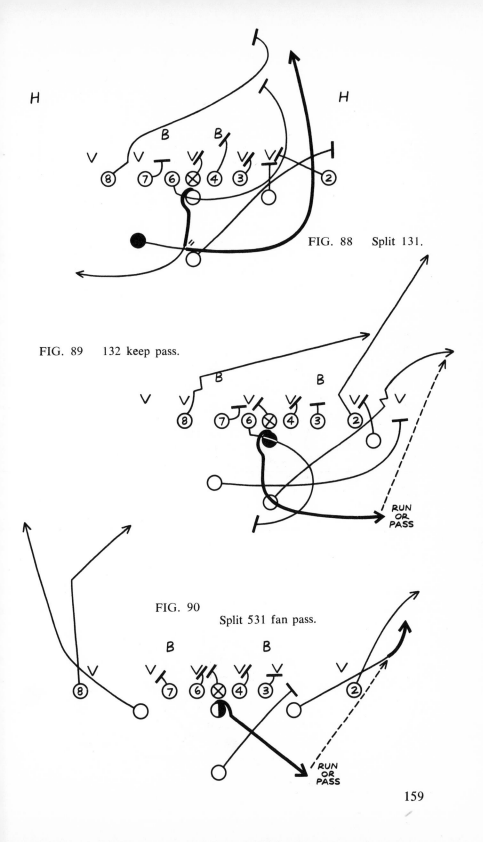

H   H

FIG. 88   Split 131.

FIG. 89   132 keep pass.

RUN
OR
PASS

FIG. 90

Split 531 fan pass.

RUN
OR
PASS

159

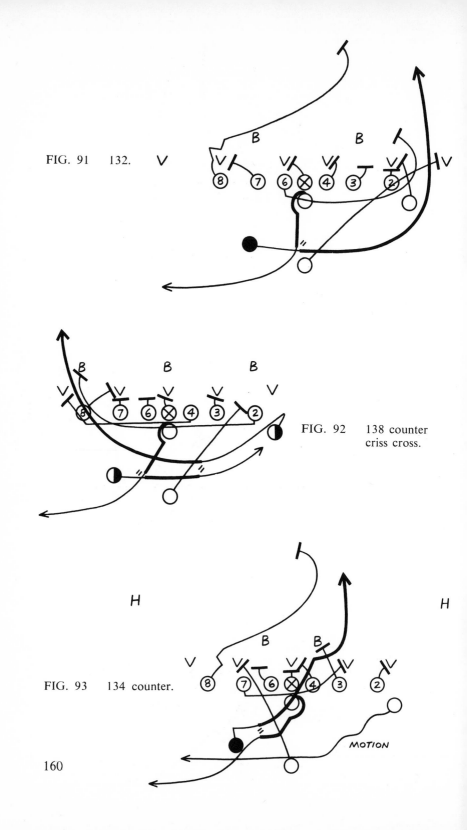

FIG. 91   132.

FIG. 92   138 counter criss cross.

FIG. 93   134 counter.

160

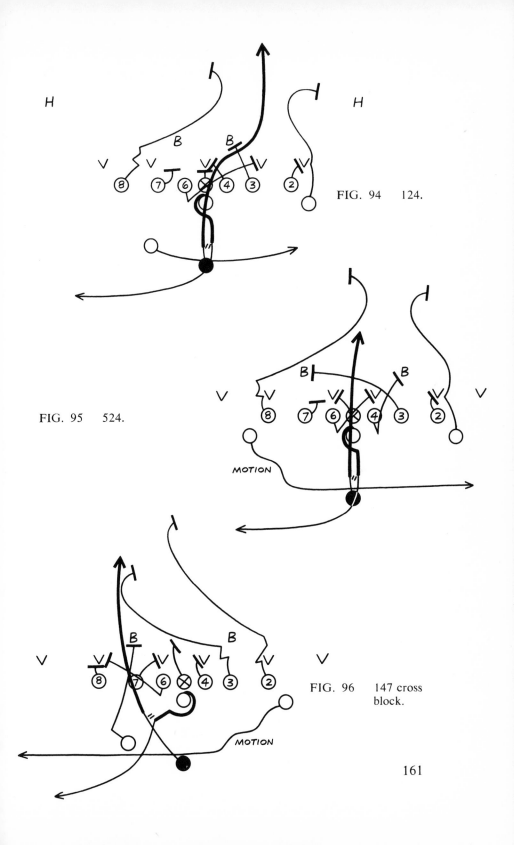

H   H

FIG. 94   124.

FIG. 95   524.

MOTION

FIG. 96   147 cross
block.

MOTION

161

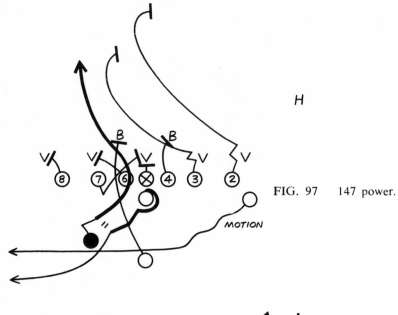

FIG. 97   147 power.

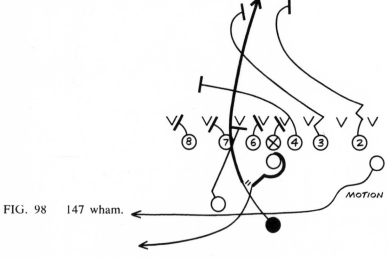

FIG. 98   147 wham.

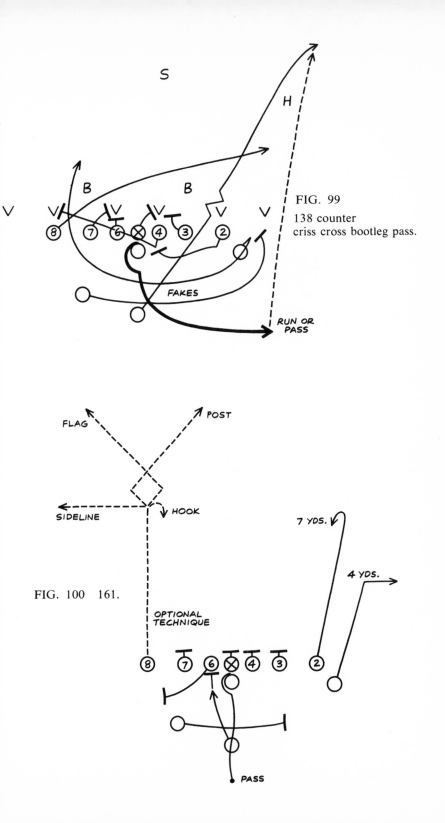

S

H

FIG. 99
138 counter
criss cross bootleg pass.

B   B

V   V   V   V   V   V

⑧   ⑦   ⑥   ⊗   ④   ③   ②

FAKES

RUN OR
PASS

FLAG   POST

SIDELINE   HOOK

7 YDS.

4 YDS.

FIG. 100   161.

OPTIONAL
TECHNIQUE

⑧   ⑦   ⑥   ⊗   ④   ③   ②

PASS

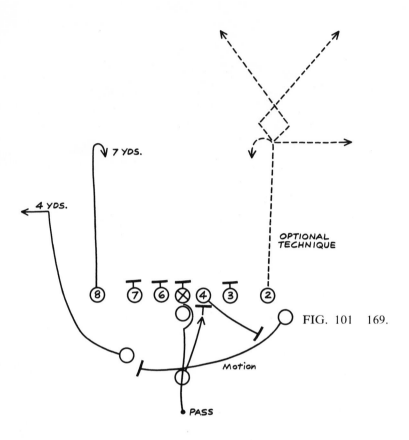

FIG. 101   169.

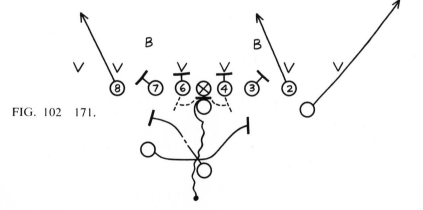

FIG. 102   171.

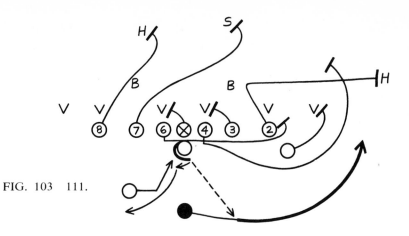

FIG. 103   111.

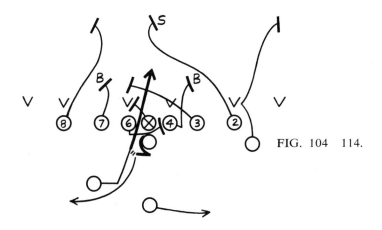

FIG. 104   114.

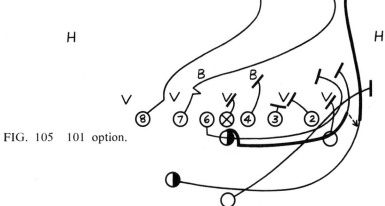

FIG. 105   101 option.

CHAPTER TEN

Maryland's
Shifty I Formation

Tom Nugent
University of Maryland

TOM NUGENT is often referred to as the "magician" of football in the South. His football innovations, considered to be the finest and most exciting by the coaching fraternity, have brought V. M. I., Florida State, and now Maryland, from near-obscurity to success through winning seasons. It was the sharp-minded Nugent who engineered and presented to football the now-famous I formation, the typewriter huddle, and the double quarterback.

Nugent has given Maryland and its fans the most interesting and most exciting football that has ever been seen in Maryland's Byrd Stadium. By combining the imaginative and successful I formation with many T formation variations, Nugent has produced the type of football that the players like to play and the fans want to see. It is wide-open football at its best.

Jim Minter of the *Atlanta Journal* once summed up the Nugent story when he wrote, "Sometimes when you talk with Tom Nugent you feel as though Mike Todd is still with us." And Minter was right. Nugent, in the energetic and colossal style of the late Mike Todd, does things first class.

Maryland's Shifty I Formation

The I formation was devised at the Virginia Military Institute in 1949. At that time we began experimenting with the formation in hopes of developing a good power off-tackle sequence to use against our opponents. With the off-tackle series as the basis of our attack that year, V. M. I. tied with Jim Tatum's Maryland team for the Southern Conference championship. This was before the division and formation of the new Atlantic Coast Conference.

Realizing then that the I formation had almost limitless possibilities, we added an outside series, then the powerful inside series, and finally the passing attack.

In 1951, Frank Leahy of Notre Dame called me at V. M. I. and asked if he could borrow our game films and notes on the I formation to use that year as a surprise weapon. We even staged a spring game and filmed it for him so that all of the blocking assignments and backfield maneuvering would be clear. Notre Dame's success with the I formation that year was given nationwide publicity and, of course, they were immediately credited with the development of the offense. In fact, to this day I am often asked at coaching clinics if the formation we use is the same one that was "invented" at Notre Dame.

The Strength of the I

The I is a unique formation in that its double-team blocking possibilities provide great concentration of power between the tackles. From tackle to tackle there are eight

Rodney Breedlove, one of Coach Nugent's outstanding I formation linemen at Maryland.

The I formation.

potential blockers for the ball-carrier, giving this particular offense a very powerful inside attack.

In the past, the general reaction to this power to the inside has been: "This is a very strong offense between the tackles, but it can't be consistently good on the outside." This would be true if defensive teams could line up against the I as they do against other formations. But with the tremendous concentration of power between the tackles, the defensive team has to put more defenders in the middle to stop the inside attack, thus making their defense vulnerable to the outside. Consequently, most of our games have been won with the outside series, even though the formation is considered stronger to the inside.

If a team is not prepared for the I formation, both on the outside and inside, our team can beat them. We have always supplemented it, however, with other formations that we can shift into if the I formation is being defended well. This shifting from one formation to another is what has given our offense its name, *The Shifty I.*

Backfield Personnel

In the I formation, the positions that the backs are placed in depends upon the particular talents of each individual back. At Maryland they are, from front to back, the quarterback, left halfback, right halfback, and fullback.

The quarterback's stance and ball-handling techniques are the same as that of the quarterback in any T formation, except that he uses a reverse pivot on almost every I formation play. The reverse pivot adds to the deceptiveness of the I formation, making it difficult for the defensive linebackers to locate the ball.

The left halfback is primarily a blocker, although he is often used effectively as a pass receiver, too. For the most part, his assignments are similar to those of the blocking back in the Single Wing offense.

The right halfback is usually the best open field runner in the backfield. He should be a speedy, shifty-type ball-carrier, but he does not have to be an exceptional blocker. We have been using him as a wing or flanker more and more each year.

The fullback is the most important man in the I formation backfield. He must have a combination of power and speed. Ideally, he should have the drive of a fullback until he gets past the line of scrimmage, and then the open field running ability of a halfback.

I FORMATION PLAYS

At Maryland, the I formation is the basis of our wide-open offensive attack. It is a formation that can be run straight, or with wingbacks, flankers, or split ends. The line may be balanced, or it may be unbalanced with both of the tackles or both of the guards and tackles on the same side of the center.

With the I, the play possibilities are almost limitless. Imagination on the part of the coach is the secret to success.

The Outside Series

There are five basic plays in the outside series. We call them the Trap, Roll, Choice, Knock, and Spin. Although there are many other plays in this series, we always return to these five basic bread and butter plays.

Gary Collins, all-American
end at Maryland.

FIG. 106 Trap right vs.
odd and even defenses.

Trap. In the Trap play, the quarterback pivots, hands off
to the fullback who is driving toward the inside leg of the
end, and continues running to the flat. (See Figure 106.)
The left halfback blocks the first man over or outside the
end.

Roll. The Roll play is an option run or pass, but it must
look like the Trap for as long as possible. (See Figure 107.)

The quarterback pivots and, faking a handoff to the fullback, sprints to the flat. The left halfback fakes a block on

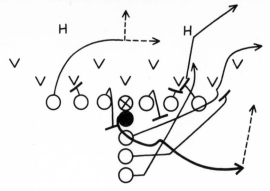

FIG. 107 Roll right vs.
odd and even defenses.

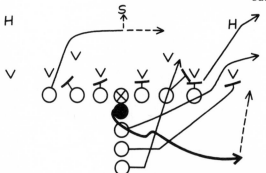

the first man over or outside the end and slides four yards deep into the flat. If the defensive corner man drops back to cover the pass, the quarterback continues running. If the cornerback comes up, the quarterback passes.

Choice. The Choice play is a quarterback belly option. (See Figure 108.)

The quarterback pivots and fakes a handoff to the fullback who runs as though he has the ball. The quarterback continues running to the flat with the right halfback outside and behind him ready for the pitch-out.

Knock. The Knock play is designed to get two blockers in front of the ball-carrier. (See Figure 109.)

The quarterback pivots, hands off to the fullback, and keeps running to the flat. The pulling guard and right halfback should reach the hole simultaneously to lead the play.

174

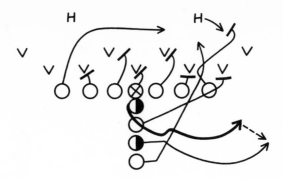

FIG. 108   Choice right vs.
            odd and even defenses.

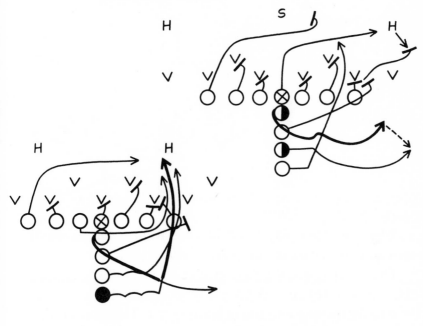

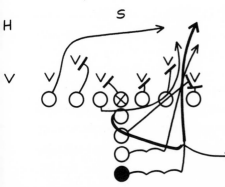

FIG. 109   Knock right vs.
            odd and even defenses.

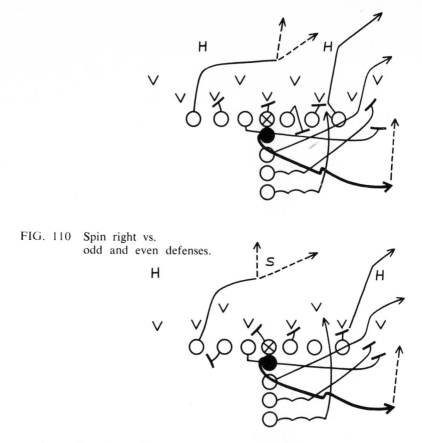

FIG. 110   Spin right vs.
odd and even defenses.

Spin. The Spin play looks like the Knock, but develops into an option pass or run. (See Figure 110.)

The quarterback pivots and fakes a handoff to the fullback. The right halfback fakes a block on the first man over or outside the end and slides into the flat. The quarterback has the option of running or throwing.

The Inside Series

The five basic inside plays are the Gut, Slant, Blast, Power, and Pop. They can be very effective plays because of the many opportunities they offer for double-team blocking.

Gut. The Gut play is good against both even and odd defenses. (See Figure 111.) The key block is by the center, who takes the defensive man whichever way he will give.

The quarterback pivots and fakes to the right halfback. He then steps backward, handing off to the fullback and continuing back to fake the pass.

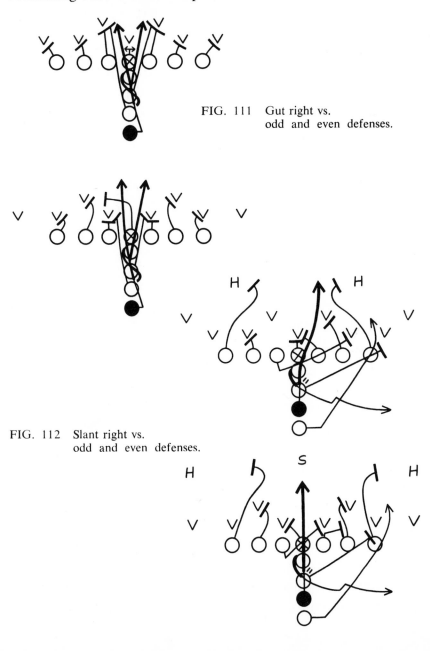

FIG. 111   Gut right vs.
odd and even defenses.

FIG. 112   Slant right vs.
odd and even defenses.

Slant. The Slant, a typical trap play, is more effective against an even than an odd defense. (See Figure 112.) It must hit quickly.

The quarterback pivots, hands off to the right halfback, and fakes a handoff to the fullback.

Blast. The Blast play provides good double-team blocking with two backs preceding the ball-carrier through the hole. (See Figure 113.) The Blast works best against a Loose Six defense.

The quarterback pivots, and, stepping backward, hands off to the fullback. The quarterback then continues back to fake the pass.

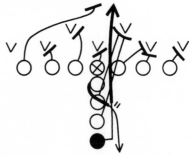

FIG. 113   Blast right vs.
            odd and even defenses.

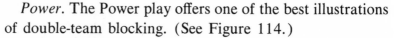

Power. The Power play offers one of the best illustrations of double-team blocking. (See Figure 114.)

The quarterback pivots and hands off to the fullback driving straight ahead. The left and right halfbacks lead the

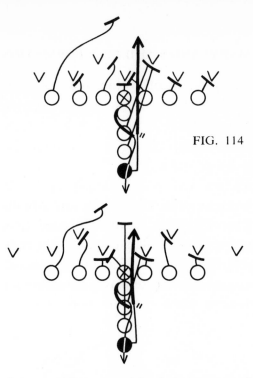

FIG. 114 Power right vs.
odd and even defenses.

play, teaming up with the center and guards to open the hole. The quarterback continues back to fake the pass.

Pop. The quick handoff or Pop play is similar to the T formation quick opener. (See Figure 115.)

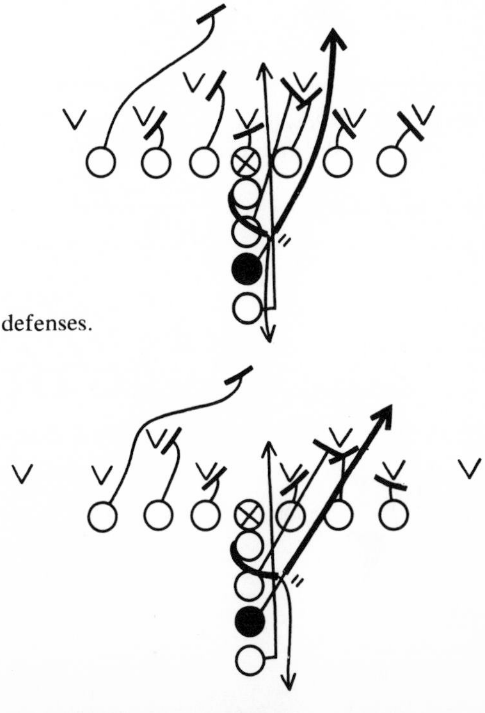

FIG. 115 Pop right vs.
odd and even defenses.

The quarterback pivots, hands off to the right halfback, fakes to the fullback, and continues back to fake the pass. The left halfback leads the play.

The Passing Game

There are many pass-play possibilities from the straight I formation, but the passing game is greatly enhanced if the coach also makes use of wingbacks, flankers, and split ends. With the many possible combinations that this offense affords, an imaginative coach can devise play passes that will raise havoc with defensive plans that are normally very sound.

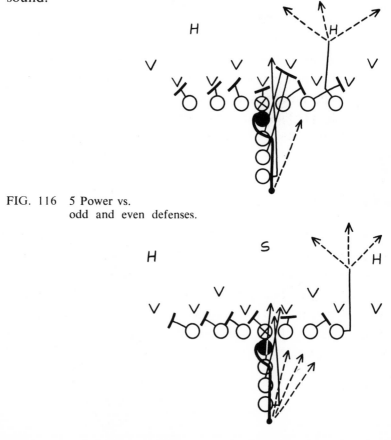

FIG. 116   5 Power vs.
            odd and even defenses.

5-Power. The inside series provides many good passing possibilities. A typical example is the 5-Power pass, which is designed to look exactly like the Power play. (See Figure 116.) Normally, only one receiver is sent out, but a delayed pass to the opposite end can be effective.

The quarterback pivots, fakes to the fullback, and, concealing the ball, fades deep to throw.

Drop Back. The Drop Back pass from the I has much the same action as a T formation drop back pass.

The right halfback and fullback block to the sides, forming a pocket of protection for the passer. The two ends and the left halfback are all possible receivers.

Flare control. We use check-offs and audible calls with our passing game to give us *swing* and *circle* routes by the protecting backs. Our quarterback can beat a blitz or heavy rush on the passer at any time through the control of these last second flare routes. In addition, we can automatic to the draw play or screen pass.

A simple pass pattern can become a most effective weapon through the addition of a swinging or circling back at just the right time.

Special Plays

Quick Kick. The I formation Quick Kick has been a very dependable weapon for us. We have never had one blocked.

As the ball is snapped to the quarterback, the deep back quickly drops back into kicking position. The halfbacks block to the sides to form a pocket for the kicker. The quarterback pivots, pitching the ball back to the kicker, and blocks to his right.

Fake Quick Kick and Pass. One of the few pass plays we have where the quarterback does not do the passing is the Fake Quick Kick and Pass.

The quarterback pivots and pitches the ball back to the fullback. Seeing this, the defensive secondary drops back quickly to receive the kick. The fullback then fakes the kick and throws to an end who is hooking in front of the secondary.

SUMMARY

The I formation and its variations afford almost countless play possibilities for the coach who believes in a wide-open style of football. Since imagination is the "key to success," it is hoped that the few suggestions offered here will help to stimulate that imagination.

CHAPTER ELEVEN

Defense: Our Kind of Football

Paul "Bear" Bryant
University of Alabama

PAUL "BEAR" BRYANT, head coach at the University of Alabama since 1958, has become famous as a rebuilder of ailing football teams. Bryant's reconstruction programs at the University of Kentucky, Texas A & M, and now Alabama, have distinguished him as one of the top coaches in the country.

During his eight years as head coach at Kentucky, Bryant pulled the Wildcats from last place in the Southeastern Conference to the top, posting an overall 60-23-5 record. At Texas A & M, Bryant began another major rebuilding job, bringing the Aggies from a 1-9 record the first year to a 24-5-2 overall record for the next three years.

When Bryant returned to his alma mater in 1958, the Crimson Tide had suffered through a dismal 4-24-2 record during the three previous seasons. In his four years at the Alabama helm, Bryant's teams have posted an impressive 31-7-5 record, winning the national championship in 1961 with a perfect 10-0 record and adding a 10-3 victory over Arkansas in the 1962 Sugar Bowl.

Selected as the 1961 Coach of the year by the American Football Coaches Association, Bryant is author of a best-selling coaching book, *Building A Championship Football Team*. (Prentice-Hall, Inc., Englewood Cliffs, N. J., 1960.)

Defense: Our Kind of Football*

Defense is one of the most important phases of football. In fact, we feel so strongly about the importance of defensive football that we spend a little more time on that phase than we do on the offensive part of the game. We feel that if we do not permit the opposition to score, we cannot lose the football game.

In order to have a good defensive team, the coach must sell his players on the importance of defensive football. I believe that our success in teaching defensive football at Alabama has been a direct result of the belief that our staff and players have in it. Defense is our kind of football.

Defensive Objectives

The primary objective of defensive football is to keep the opposition from scoring. We want our players to feel that their ultimate goal is to keep the opposition from crossing our goal line.

Secondly, our kicking game must be sound. We must be able to kick the ball safely out of dangerous territory. Providing we do this, and are able to eliminate the "easy" touchdown (the long pass or long run for six points), we believe our opposition's own offense will stop itself 65 per cent of the time through a broken signal, a penalty, or some other offensive mistake. Therefore, if our boys are aggres-

---

* From *Building a Championship Football Team* by Paul "Bear" Bryant (Englewood Cliffs, N. J.: Prentice-Hall, Inc., 1960), Chap. 4.

sive while on defense, we should be able to keep the opposition from scoring about 25 per cent of the time they have the ball. The remaining 10 per cent will be a dog fight. Therefore, we must instill in our defensive men a fierce competitive pride that each player is personally responsible for keeping the opposition from scoring.

The Offensive-Minded Defense

The next objective is to sell the players on the idea that our defensive unit can and will score for us. There are more ways to score while on defense than on offense; consequently, the odds favor the defense. If statistics are kept on the defensive team's performance, and the defensive team is given credit for all scores made by running back punts, recovering fumbles, or any other defensive maneuvers where they either score or get the ball inside the opposition's 25-yard line resulting in a score, the players can be sold on the idea of the offensive-minded defense.

Defense—A Team Proposition

A sound defense is one that has every player on defense carrying out his assignment. Then it is impossible for the offense to score. Note that I said every player, which makes defense a team proposition and eliminates the individual defensive play. By this we mean that every defense is coordinated and each player is an important part of the overall defensive unit. We try to instill in every boy that he is personally responsible to see that the opposition does not score. When individual players and a team accept this responsibility, we feel that we are making progress and are beginning to build a winner.

Offensive football is assignment football, while defense is reaction football. One mistake on defense can cost a team a football game. Consequently there cannot be errors on defense. To eliminate errors, you must always have the strength of your defense against the strength of the offense. The defensive players must be positioned in such a way that the team as a whole can handle any situation that might arise.

We do not believe you can teach defensive football successfully unless you are able to present a clear picture to your players of what you are trying to accomplish. Our objective is to limit the offense to as small an area as possible. By limiting their attack, we can hem them in and catch them. We attempt to build a fence around the ball, and around the offensive operation. We want our players to have a picture of exactly how we are going to build this fence, and what we hope to accomplish, both of which will be explained later.

Sell Them On Defensive Football

In defensive football, every play is a personal challenge. When on defense, the players are challenging the offensive players in relating to an area of ground or field. Every man should believe, "I am not going to let the offense score." If you expect to be a winner, either as a player or a coach, you must believe this philosophy 100 per cent. Your play must be sound, and you must believe in it.

We want to make our defensive players believe that when the opposing team has the ball inside our 3-yard line they aren't going to score—they can't score—they must not score! If a team believes this, it is almost impossible for the offense to score. In 1950 our defensive unit prevented opposing teams from scoring on 19 occasions from the 3-yard line. The morale of the defensive players was outstanding. They thought it was impossible for another team to score on them even though they had only three yards to defend. I recall in our game with Oklahoma University in the Sugar Bowl, the Sooners got down to our 3-yard line. We were caught with three or four of our best players on the bench, and we were trying to get them back into the game quickly. As Jim McKenzie, who had been replaced, came off the field, he said, "Don't worry, Coach, they will never score on us." And they did not score! When I see such evidence as this, I know our players believe what we tell them, and "we are in business!"

We sell our boys on the idea that playing defense is the toughest assignment in football. We try to see to it that our defensive players get a lot of the recognition and favorable publicity. If our defense makes a goal line stand and we win the game, we try to give the defensive players much of the recognition.

Gang Tackling—A Defensive Must

During all phases of our defensive work we elaborate frequently on the importance of gang tackling. We like to see six or seven of our boys in on every tackle. Such tactics are not only demoralizing to ball-carriers and wear them down physically, but represent sound football. It is difficult for the ball-carrier to break loose and score when half a dozen men are fighting to get a piece of him.

We want the first tackler to get a good shot at the ball carrier, making certain he does not miss him. We want the other defenders to "tackle the ball," and make the ball carrier fumble it so we can get possession of the football. We are trying to get possession of the football any way we can.

Frankly, we want the first man to the ball carrier merely to hold him up, and not let him get away, so we can unload on him. You can punish a ball-carrier when one man has him "dangling," and the others gang tackle him hard. I am not implying that we want our boys to pile on and play dirty football merely to get a ball-carrier out of the game. First, we do not teach this type of football as it is a violation of the rules and spirit of the game. Second, piling on brings a 15-yard penalty. We cannot win when we get penalized in clutch situations.

FIVE-SPOKE DEFENSE

The 5-spoke or 3-deep, as it is often called, is a very sound defense in the secondary. In the 5-spoke defense, we compare the perimeter of our defensive secondary to one-half of a wheel which has five spokes. (See Figure 117.)

At the end of each of the imaginary spokes is a defender. The spokes can be lengthened or shortened, but they can not be brought closer together or there will be a vulnerable area in the defensive secondary.

As illustrated in Figure 117, there are defensive men stationed at the ends of the spokes at points 1, 2, 3, 4, and 5. The defensive end located at 1 covers the area from point F to A; the halfback at point 2 covers the area from A to B; the safety at point 3 covers the area from B to C; the halfback at point 4 covers C to D; and the end at point 5

FIG. 117

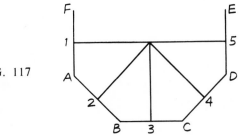

covers the area from D to E. If the length of the spokes is
decreased, the area to be covered will not be as great. Conversely, the longer the spokes, the greater the area to be
covered by the defensive secondary. If we stretch a wire
from F to A to B to C to D to E, the area enclosed repre-
sents the space in which we should be able to contain our
opponents.

The half-wheel will revolve clockwise and counter-clockwise, but the defenders must always remain at their points
at the end of the spokes, keeping the same relative distance
from each other. If the offensive team runs to their left, the
wheel should revolve to our right, counter-clockwise, as is
illustrated in Figure 118. It would be just the opposite if
the play were run to our left. If it were a running play up-
the-middle, the spokes of the wheel would shorten as the
defensive men converged on the ball carrier, keeping their
same proportionate distances from each other.

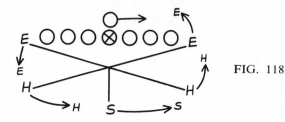

FIG. 118

On a pass play, the length of the spokes are determined
by the distance of the defenders from the passer. For example, if the passer goes back to throw a "drop back" pass,
the spokes should stretch proportionately. The defenders
would have time to cover more distance if the passer attempts to throw deep because the ball must remain in the
air longer in order to reach the receiver. Conversely, if the
passer attempts to throw a quick pass from only a yard or
so off the line of scrimmage, the receivers will not have

time to get deep; consequently the length of the spokes will be shortened proportionately when the defenders converge on the ball as it is thrown.

FOUR-SPOKE DEFENSE

The 4-spoke or 2-deep is also a very good defense, although it requires better athletes to play some of its positions. We would probably be using the 4-spoke defense today if it were not for the number of teams we play that quick kick frequently. This was a major factor in our changing from the 4-spoke defense which we used successfully at Texas A & M to the 5-spoke defense which we now use at the University of Alabama.

The principle of the 4-spoke defense is basically the same as that of the 5-spoke, except that there are only four men in the outer perimeter of the secondary. The spokes run from an imaginary center with a defender placed on the end of each spoke, as is illustrated in Figure 119.

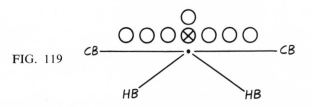

FIG. 119

OUR DEFENSIVE NUMBERING SYSTEM
AND TERMINOLOGY

After coaching for a number of years, and always trying to find something that would make football easier to understand for the average player, I came upon a system of defensive numbering that has proved very valuable to me. In the past we had used many different defenses and had always given each defense a name. Most of the time the name had little in common with the defense, and this confused, rather than helped, the players. After discussing the possibility of the numbering system with my own coaches and other college and high school coaches, I finally came across a feasible plan for numbering defensive alignments. I must give credit to O. A. "Bum" Phillips, a Texas high school coach, for helping to work out the solution with his high school team.

In the numbering of our defense now, we give a number to each offensive man, as well as to the gaps between the offensive linemen. (See Figure 120.)

FIG. 120

Accompanying each number is a particular "technique." If a defensive player lines up in a 2 position, he will play what we call a "2 technique;" a 3 position plays a "3 technique," etc. Therefore, we line up our defensive men from one end of the offensive line to the other, and each position has a particular technique.

Each linebacker calls the defense for his particular side of the line. He controls his guard, tackle and himself, but he does not control the end on his side of the line. The latter is controlled by the defensive signal caller in the secondary who gives a call for the 4- or 5-spoke defensive alignment.

Each linebacker calls two numbers. The first number tells his guard where to line up and his accompanying defensive technique. The second number gives the same information to the defensive tackle.

For example, if the linebacker calls, "26," the guard plays a 2 technique and the tackle a 6 technique. If the caller says, "59," the guard plays a 5 technique and the tackle a 9 technique. When the linebacker tells the guard and tackle which techniques to play through his oral call, he

FIG. 121

then lines up in a position to cover the remaining gaps. For example, Figure 121 illustrates a 26 call. The linebacker must take a position between his guard and tackle so he can fill the gaps not covered by the other front defenders. You can see by this example that the linebacker is in a position to help out over the offensive tackle position, and also on wide plays to his side of the line.

FIG. 122

Figure 122 illustrates the position of the defensive right guard, tackle, and linebacker when the call is 59. The linebacker is now in a position to help out on a play that is in the middle of the line.

If we are playing a 4-spoke defense, we assign one defender to play "head on" the offensive center, and he does not figure in any of the calls. He lines up the same every time, as is illustrated in Figure 123.

FIG. 123

When we play a 5-spoke defense, the two linebackers assign one player to the area inside the offensive guards. For example, if we are playing a 5-spoke defense and the call on the right side is 59, the call on the left side must have a 1

FIG. 124

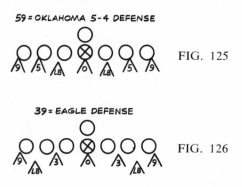

as the first digit, such as 17, 16, or 15. Figure 124 illustrates a 59 call on the right and a 17 call on the left. The man playing the 1 technique on the left is necessary in order to keep from having a large gap between the two guards.

By having our players learn only a few numbers and their accompanying techniques, we can line up in numerable defensive alignments by merely calling two numbers. Figures 125 and 126 are example of 59 and 39 defensive calls, which are commonly referred to as the Oklahoma and Eagle defenses, respectively. Each is a 4-spoke defense with a man in a 0 technique.

59 = OKLAHOMA 5-4 DEFENSE

FIG. 125

39 = EAGLE DEFENSE

FIG. 126

Figure 127 illustrates a 25 call, with a 0 technique, and is a 9-man front defensive alignment.

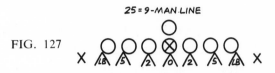

FIG. 127

Figures 128—130 are 5-spoke defenses representing 26, 37, and 13 calls. These are commonly referred to as a wide tackle 6, a split 6, and a gap 8, respectively.

The defenses shown in Figures 125—130 happen to have the same call to each side, but remember that each side is independent of the other as far as the calls are concerned. To eliminate any confusion, merely designate which side is to call first, and the other linebacker can adjust on his call accordingly so that there is not a large gap in the middle of the defensive line. The linebackers must be especially aware of this if we are employing a 5-spoke defensive alignment.

The signal caller should never call a defense involving two successive numbers, such as 2-3 or 7-6, as this will

FIG. 128

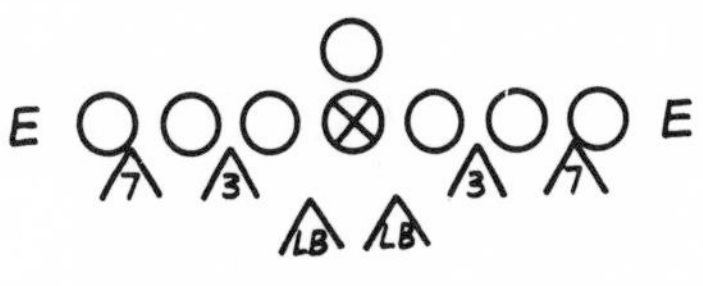

FIG. 129

FIG. 130

leave too much territory for the linebacker to try to cover. The caller is always responsible for having a man in, or capable of covering, every gap.

It is very simple for the defensive signal caller to change the guard and tackle assignments even after he has given them a position to line up in. The caller merely adds a zero (0) or a one (1) to the end of the number he has called. For example, if he gives the call 37 and he wants the players in the 3 technique to charge one-half a man toward the inside, he says, "30." If he wants this defender to charge one-half a man to the outside, he says, "31." This second call is given to only one player at a time, but he can change both of their techniques by saying "31-71" or "30-70," etc.

Employing a defensive numbering system requires alert defensive signal callers. They must be aware of the tactical situation at all times, and must call a sound defense according to tactical and strategical planning. For example, a good short yardage call would be 13, and sound passing situation calls would be 36, 37, 39, and 59.

Our present system is the simplest method I know of for getting players into various defenses quickly and with a minimum amount of talking. We feel it eliminates much confusion during the game. And, in practice when a coach is discussing the different defensive situations, he can refer to the particular techniques and immediately everyone understands the defensive alignment.

Playing Our Defensive Techniques

As illustrated in Figure 120, our techniques and defensive positions are numbered from 0 to 9 on both sides of the defensive line.

The 0 Technique. The defender employing the 0 technique lines up head on the offensive centers. (See Figure
131.) On a short yardage situation he lines up close to the
center's head. On a long yardage situation, he is usually
about one yard off the ball. His technique is to play the
center's head with a quick hand shiver at the snap of the
ball. When he makes contact with the center, he brings his

FIG. 131

back foot up so his feet are even with each other. If the
quarterback goes straight back to pass, the 0 technique man
is responsible for the draw play, and then he rushes the
passer. If it is a run instead of a pass, he keeps the center
away from his blocking surface, not permitting himself to be
tied up in the middle of the line, and he pursues the ball
taking his proper angle, depending on the type of running
play it is.

The 1 Technique. The main job of the player employing
the 1 technique is to control the offensive splits, forcing the
guards to keep their splits to a minimum. (See Figure 132.)
He is also responsible for keeping the center off the defensive linebacker. If both guards are playing in this technique,
as is illustrated in Figure 132, only one will "slam" the center, while the other takes a long step toward his guard, playing him from the inside out. He must always be aware of

FIG. 132

the trap from the inside. If the play is a back-up pass, he is responsible for the draw first, and rushing the passer second. If it is a running play, he slams the center or guard and pursues the football.

The 2 Technique. The 2 technique is similar to the 0 technique. (See Figure 133.) One difference is that the guard is head on the offensive guard, instead of on the offensive center. The distance he lines up off the ball is determined by the tactical situation. On the snap of the ball

FIG. 133

he plays the guard with a hand shiver, and immediately locates the football. If it is a back-up pass and there is no man in a 0 or 1 technique, he looks for a draw play first, and then rushes the passer. If it is a running play, he looks first toward the inside for a trap, and then pursues the football.

The 3 Technique. The 3 technique is similar to the 1 technique. (See Figure 134.) The 3 man is responsible for keeping the offensive tackle's split cut down, and on occasion, to keep the offensive guard or tackle from blocking the defensive linebacker. When the ball is snapped, the 3 technique man plays either the guard or tackle, depending upon the defense, with a quick flipper or shiver with the hands. He is to watch for the trap at all times. If the play

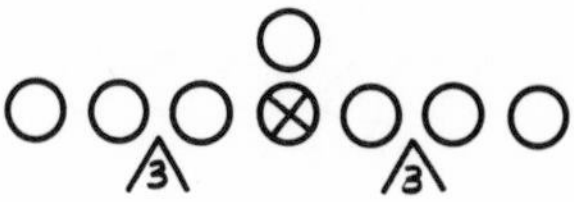

FIG. 134

is a straight drop back pass, he rushes the passer from the inside. If it is a running play, he pursues the football.

The 4 Technique. The 4 technique man lines up head on the offensive tackle, about twelve to eighteen inches off the ball. (See Figure 135.) On the snap of the ball he plays the offensive tackle with a quick hand shiver or forearm flipper. If it is a running play toward him, he must first whip the offensive tackle, and then be ready to stop the hand-off or help out on the off-tackle play. If it is a straight back-up

FIG. 135

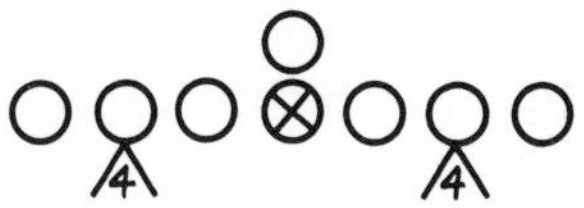

pass, he rushes the passer from the inside. If the play goes to the opposite side, he must control the offensive tackle and pursue the football.

The 5 Technique. The 5 technique man lines up on the outside eye of the offensive tackle. (See Figure 136.) On the snap of the ball he employs a forearm flip charge into the tackle. He has 75 per cent off-tackle responsibility, and he should never be blocked in by only one man. If the play comes toward the 5 man, he must be certain to keep the offensive blocker in front of him, as he will be eliminated from the play very easily if he tries to go around his blocker. If it is a straight back-up pass, he rushes the passer from the inside out. If the play goes away from him, he must pursue the football.

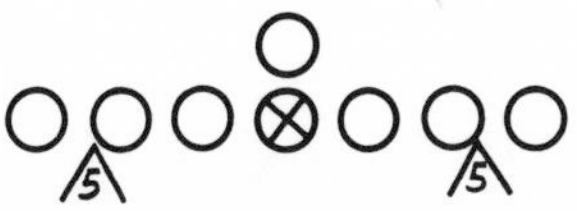

FIG. 136

The 6 Technique. The 6 technique player lines up head on the offensive end. (See Figure 137.) If the end splits too far, the 6 man is to "shoot the gap." He is primarily responsible for keeping the offensive end from releasing quickly on passes and for keeping the end from blocking the linebacker. He is also responsible for stopping the off-tackle play. The game situation will determine how far he lines up off the ball, but it usually varies from one to three yards. If the play comes toward the 6 man, he whips the end with a flip or shiver charge, and helps out both inside and outside. If it is an option play toward him, he must make the quarterback pitch the ball or he must tackle the

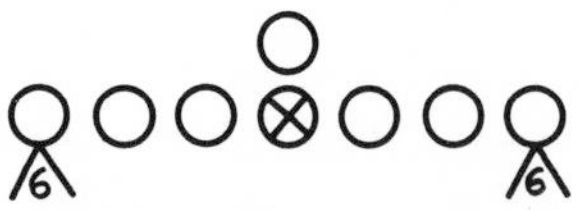

FIG. 137

quarterback. When the flow is away from him, he trails the play, staying as deep as the deepest man in the offensive backfield, so he can contain the reverse play back to his side. If the play is a straight back pass, the 6 man is responsible for rushing the passer from the outside in.

The 7 Technique. The 7 technique player lines up splitting the inside foot of the offensive end. (See Figure 138.) He is responsible for forcing the end to reduce his offensive split. He has 75 per cent inside responsibility and 25 per cent outside responsibility. When the ball is snapped, he uses a hand or forearm flipper charge on the offensive end. His main responsibility is to whip the offensive end, and

FIG. 138

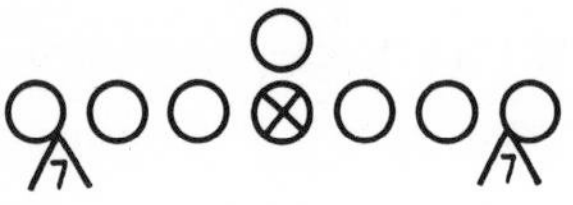

close the off-tackle play. He must never be blocked by the
end. If the play is a straight drop back pass, he is the outside rusher and must not let the quarterback get outside
him. If the play goes away from him, he is to trail the ball
carrier, staying as deep as the deepest offensive backfield
man so he can contain any reverse coming back to his side
of the line.

The 8 Technique. When we speak of a man playing an 8
technique, we are speaking of a "true end," a defensive end
who lines up outside the offensive end. (See Figure 139.)
The 8 man's position is from one and one-half to three
yards outside the offensive end's normal position, with his

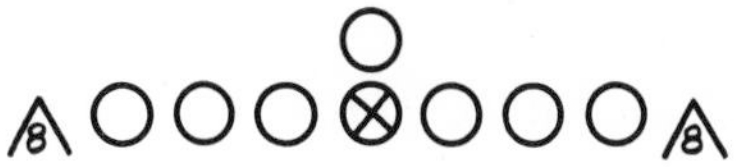

FIG. 139

inside foot forward and his shoulders parallel with the line
of scrimmage. If it is a straight back pass, the defensive
end, without taking his eyes off the passer, will turn to his
outside. Then, using a cross-over step, he sprints to his outside, trying to get width and depth to play the ball to his
side. His depth should be 8 to 10 yards, similar to a linebacker's position covering the flat. He stops running when
the quarterback stops to set up. When the ball is thrown, he
sprints for the ball.

If the play comes to the 8 man, we want him to cross the
line of scrimmage for about two yards, playing the outside
blocker. He is the outside contain man and he must not permit the ball to get outside him. He never makes the quarterback pitch the ball on option plays. If it is a running pass
toward him, he is the outside contain and rush man. If the

flow goes away from him, he must make sure it is not a reverse play back to his side before he takes his proper angle
of pursuit, which is through the area where the defensive
safety man lined up originally.

The 9 Technique. When playing a 9 technique, the defensive man splits the outside foot of the offensive end. (See
Figure 140.) He lines up 14 inches off the line of scrimmage.
When the ball is snapped, the 9 technique man takes a short
step with his inside foot toward the offensive end, and at
the same time delivers a hand or forearm shiver to the head
of the offensive end. If the offensive end blocks in and the
play comes toward him, the 9 man immediately looks for
the near halfback or the trapper, expecting to be blocked
by either of these offensive men.

If a running play comes toward him and the quarterback
is going to option the football, the 9 man must make the
quarterback pitch the ball. If the quarterback is faking the
ball to the fullback, the 9 man must "search" the fullback
for the ball first.

The 9 technique man never crosses the line of scrimmage.
If the offensive play is a straight back pass, he delivers a
blow to the end, and then drops back two or three yards
looking for the screen or short pass. He is in position to
come up and make the tackle if the quarterback gets outside
of the rusher and decides to run with the ball. If the flow
goes away, the 9 man trails and has the same responsibilities as the 6 and 7 technique men.

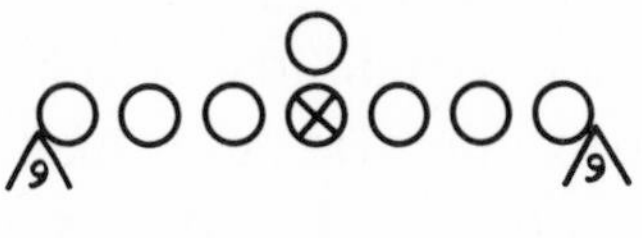

FIG. 140

DEFENSIVE STANCE

We want our defensive men to be comfortable, but at the same time they must be in a position to uncoil, make good contact, and then be in position to move quickly. We never permit a man to take a stance in which he gets too extended and loses most of his hitting power. There are a few basic techniques that we insist our defensive players use. These techniques vary to some extent from position to position.

Guards—The guards take a four-point stance with their feet even and spread about three inches wider than their shoulders. Their weight must be slightly forward, with the tail slightly higher than the shoulders. The guard's back is straight and his shoulders are square. His hands are a bit wider than his feet, with thumbs turned in and slightly ahead of his shoulders.

Tackles—The tackles take a four-point stance with their feet spread a little wider than their shoulders and the inside foot staggered back slightly. Their body weight must be forward slightly and the tail should be a little higher than the head. Their backs are straight, their shoulders square, and their necks must be relaxed. The hands are slightly outside of the feet, with thumbs turned in slightly ahead of their shoulders.

Ends—The defensive ends line up in a good football position with their inside foot forward and perpendicular to the line of scrimmage. The knees are bent and their bodies are bent forward slightly at the waist. The ends must have their eyes on the quarterback, but still be able to see the offensive halfback and end closest to them on their side. When the action starts toward an end, we want him to come across the line and make contact with the outside blocker. The shoulders should remain parallel with the line of scrimmage upon contact with an offensive back.

Linebackers—The linebackers stand with their feet even and parallel with each other. They should be in a good football position—tail down, back straight, slight bend at the waist, weight on the balls of the feet, and knees bent. The

Lee Roy Jordan, all-American tackle at Alabama.

linebacker takes a step forward with the inside foot toward the blocker who is firing out at him. He then brings his back foot up even with his forward foot so that he will be in a position to move laterally.

Halfbacks—The defensive halfbacks line up in their regular position, which is three yards outside of the offensive end in the 5-spoke defense, and on the inside shoulder of the offensive end in the 4-spoke defense. We want our halfbacks to have their outside foot back with the inside foot pointing perpendicular to the line of scrimmage. The outside foot is about 14 inches behind the front foot, and pointing out at a 45 degree angle. The halfback's knees should be flexed slightly, and he must be in a good football position. His arms should be in a cocked position. He faces the quarterback. His first step is backward and outward.

Corner Men—The corner man lines up in his regular position about four yards wide and two and a half yards deep. His feet are parallel and even, about 18 inches apart, pointing directly toward the offensive quarterback. He should be in a good football position, weight on the balls of the feet, arms cocked, etc. He should not rest his hands on his knees. From a good football position he can rotate quickly and properly, or he can come forward and meet the play if it comes toward him.

Safety—The safety man lines up a little deeper than any other backs. He is turned slightly toward the wide side of the field or the strong side of the offensive backfield. He has his outside foot back, and he is permitted to stand a little straighter than the other deep backs. He, too, is in a good football position watching the quarterback. He must be able to cover a pass from sideline to sideline.

OUR SURPRISE DEFENSE

We never send our boys into a football game without trying to prepare them for every situation that might arise during the contest. We must try to anticipate every situation,
and counteract with a sound defense. A situation might be
very unusual, and we cannot actually defense it properly
until the coach in the press box tells us exactly what the
opposition is doing. Then we can work out the proper defense on the sideline and send it in. In the meantime the
boys must have something they can counteract with immediately or the opposition is likely to score with its surprise offense. Consequently our signal caller yells "Surprise
Defense!" when he sees an unusual offensive formation, and
the boys react accordingly. Our rules for covering a spread
or unusual offensive alignment are as follows:

1. If one man flanks, our halfback covers him.
2. If two men go out, our halfback and end move out
   and cover them.
3. If three men go out, our halfback, end and tackle
   move out and cover them.
4. If four offensive men go out, we put out the halfback, end and tackle, and our linebacker goes out
   half-way. The linebacker's position is then a yard
   deeper than usual.
5. If five or more men go out, we put out the halfback,
   end, tackle, and guard, with the linebacker going
   only half-way.
6. If there is any doubt about how to meet strength
   with strength, we start with the outside man and put
   a defender on every other offensive player.

7. The safety man will always play in the middle of the field or in the middle of the eligible pass receivers.

8. A defensive end must never be flanked by one offensive man unless he can beat the flanker through the gap into the offensive backfield.

9. A tackle should never be flanked by two offensive men unless he can beat the nearest opponent through the gap.

10. The initial charge of the players who are left on defense is to the outside, unless there is a concentration of the offensive backs. If that is the case, then the defensive charge will be normal.

11. The greater the offensive team splits its line, the farther off the line of scrimmage the defenders must play.

Figures 141 and 142 illustrate two examples of spread formations, and applications of our *surprise defense* coverage rules.

The first offensive man who flanks to our right (Figure 141), is covered by our defensive right halfback. The second to our right is covered by our right end. The first man flanked to our left is covered by our defensive left halfback; the second man out, by our left end; the third flanker, by our left tackle; the fourth flanker is covered by our left linebacker, who moves out half-way. The fifth man flanked to

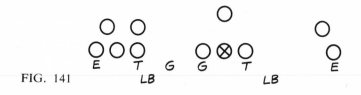

FIG. 141

our left is covered by our left guard. The remaining players meet strength with strength. Our right guard plays on the outside shoulder of the offensive right guard, and the defensive right tackle plays on the outside shoulder of the offensive left guard.

We instruct our defensive players to force the offensive players to come to them. We do not want our men off the line of scrimmage to penetrate, leaving gaps in the defense.

Figure 142 illustrates another example of the application of our *surprise defense* rules in covering a spread offense.

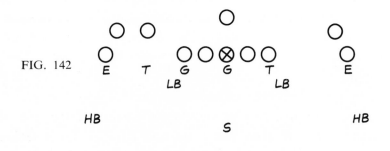

FIG. 142

OUR VICTORY DEFENSE

It is very important for a team to be able to go into a *Victory Defense* when they hold a slim lead with little time remaining before the termination of the first half or the game. We go into a 5-man line if we have the game won and our opponents are not close to our goal line. Under such circumstances we can afford to permit the opposition to get a first down or two, but we cannot afford to let them complete the long pass or the long run for a touchdown. We believe our victory defense is sound, and that we are playing

sound defensive football when we employ it. Figure 143 illustrates the victory defense we used eight times in one year,
and we intercepted our opposition's intended forward pass
on seven of the eight occasions.

The individual and team duties and responsibilities when
we employ our *Victory Defense* are as follows:

Middle Lineman—He looks for the screen pass and/or
the draw play.

Ends and Tackles—They line up on the outside shoulder
of the offensive ends and tackles. If the offensive ends split,
we adjust on them with our deep backs. We want our defensive ends to shove the offensive ends to the inside, holding them up if possible, and then to look to the inside for a
trap block or for a screen pass. Should neither of these occur, the ends are to contain the passer, not permitting him
to get outside either of their respective positions. They
should play loose and proceed with caution, rather than
rushing hard into the offensive backfield.

The defensive tackles should play back off the line of
scrimmage with their feet even and parallel. Each tackle

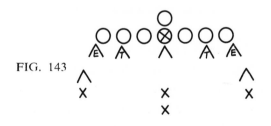

FIG. 143

must keep his man in front of him, not permitting the offensive tackle to block him in or out. When a pass develops,
the tackle rushes the passer, making certain to stay in front
of the football.

Linebackers—They line up about six yards deep and at a spot opposite where the defensive end would ordinarily line up. By lining up wide, we hope to funnel the offense toward the middle of our formation. By this I mean we want them to direct their attack toward the inside. They must not get outside the defense or kill the clock by running out-of-bounds.

Halfbacks and Safety—They line up at least 12 yards deep. The halfbacks stay well outside the offensive formation and the safety man is in the middle of the defensive alignment. The three backs play their regular defense.

Best Defensive Player—The next step in setting up our *Victory Defense* is to station our very best defensive football player 10 yards behind the middle safety man. His sole responsibility is to keep the offensive team from scoring. He must always stay between the ball and the goal line. We do not want him to come forward and break up a pass. Nor do we want him coming up to make a tackle. We want him to fight off blockers and make certain the ball carrier does not score if the opposition moves downfield with a long run or a completed pass. When the ball is thrown, we want every man on the team to go for the ball *except* our deepest man. He remains 10 yards behind the ball at all times in case there is a tip that the opponent might catch and carry over for the score.

OUR GOAL LINE DEFENSE

When we go into our goal line defense, we want our boys to be so completely sold on what they are doing that they are not going to let the opposition score. Each man must take it upon himself to see that they do not score over his

Billy Neighbors, all-American guard at Alabama.

particular defensive area. Playing goal line defense is a terrific challenge. There is not much territory remaining, and the big questions are, "Who is going to come out on top?" and "Who will end up with the ball when the dust settles?" If we give our team a sound plan and teach it to them well, and if they believe in it and in us, we will do all right.

Figure 144 illustrates our goal line defense. The individual and team duties and responsibilities are as follows:

FIG. 144

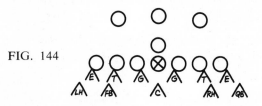

Ends—The defensive ends line up in a four-point stance as close to the line of scrimmage as they can get, just shading the outside eyes of the offensive ends. On the snap of the ball the defensive ends charge low and hard through the tail of their offensive ends, trying to get approximately one yard deep into the offensive backfield. If the flow comes toward his side and the quarterback has the football, the defensive end tries to force the quarterback to pitch back to the off-halfback.

Tackles—The defensive tackles line up on the outside eyes of the offensive tackles and aim for a spot one yard deep in the offensive backfield, behind the inside foot of the offensive tackles. Each tackle is responsible for the hand-off play to his side. He must either make the tackle or force the dive play to the inside so the middle linebacker can make the tackle.

Guards—The defensive guards get their spacing by lining up on each other, but theoretically they line up on the

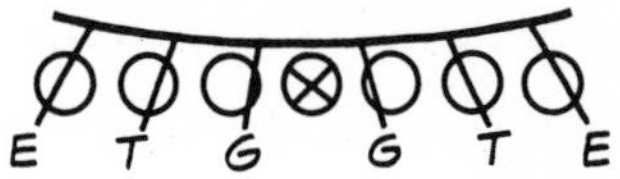

FIG. 145

E T G G T E

inside eyes of the offensive guards. They are responsible for sealing off the middle of the line, and for keeping the offensive center from blocking the middle linebacker. They aim for a spot about one yard behind the offensive center's position, using a low, hard submarine charge.

If our six linemen carry out their defensive assignments using a low, hard charge and get to their predetermined spots, we will then form a wall. (See Figure 145.)

Middle Linebacker or Defensive Center—He is responsible for making any play that occurs between the offensive tackles. He should make the tackle on a hand-off or on a play up the middle, and should help on the off-tackle play. On a back-up pass, he drops back to cover a short zone. If the play starts wide, the middle linebacker pursues the football. He should be one of the best defensive football players. Figure 146 illustrates the defensive position and responsibilities of the middle linebacker.

FIG. 146

C

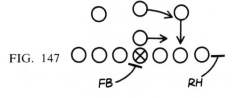

FIG. 147

FB   RH

Inside Linebackers—They are responsible for the off-tackle play and the quick containing of the quarterback on the option play. (See Figure 147.) If the flow goes away, they check for the counter play before they pursue the football. On a running pass, as illustrated in Figure 148, one linebacker covers the flat and the other his hook spot. On a back-up pass they cover the short one-quarter zones.

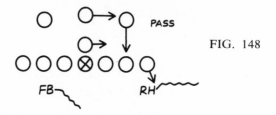

FIG. 148

Outside Linebackers—They are responsible for the wide play. They must not permit the play to get outside them on their particular sides of the defensive alignment. When the offensive play starts, both outside linebackers "read" the offensive end closest to them, and the flow of the offensive backs. It is important that they diagnose a running pass correctly, because the offensive end to the on-side must be covered correctly if his route is deep. (The outside linebacker must cover the deep man whether it's an end or a back.) If the play is away, the backs revolve toward it.

The two inside and two outside linebackers play 4-spoke pass coverage on all passes.

A SPLIT T DEFENSE

There are a number of good defenses that can be used against a T team with a straight-up T backfield. Figure 149

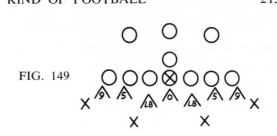

FIG. 149

illustrates our 59 call or the Oklahoma 5-4 defense versus the T formation. The individual and team duties and responsibilities are as follows:

Ends—The defensive ends play a 9 technique, and on this particular defense, both ends' assignments and techniques are identical. They do not penetrate beyond the line of scrimmage unless the flow is away. When the flow goes away, the off-side defensive end becomes the trail man.

Tackles—The defensive tackles play a 5 technique. They never cross the line except on straight drop back passes, and then both tackles rush the passer. Otherwise the tackles whip their respective opponents' (tackles) and pursue the football.

Middle Guard—The middle guard plays a 0 technique, always alert for the screen pass or the draw play. On the snap of the ball, the middle guard should whip the offensive center and then go to the ball.

Linebackers—The inside linebackers line up on the outside eyes of their respective offensive guards and "read" through them into the offensive backfield. If the offensive guards or tackles fire out, the linebackers whip them and go to the football. If the flow goes away, the off-side linebacker checks the counter play, and then pursues the football. On a drop back pass, each linebacker covers his short one-quarter pass zone.

Secondary—The defensive secondary plays its regular 4-spoke defense and revolves on the plays after the offense shows what they are going to do (or from a pre-determined call).

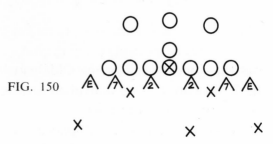

FIG. 150

Figure 150 illustrates our 27 call or a wide tackle 6 defensive alignment against the T formation. The individual and team duties and responsibilities are as follows:

Guards—The guards play a tough 2 technique, then pursue the football. On a drop back pass they are responsible for the screen pass in the middle, for the draw play, and for rushing the passer.

Tackles—The tackles play a tough 7 technique. They are responsible for the off-tackle play to their respective sides. If the play goes away, the tackle is the trail man. On back-up passes, the tackles rush the passer from the outside.

Ends—The defensive ends play an 8 technique, and they are the contain men if the flow comes their way. If the ball goes away, the off-end drops back and pursues through the area where the safety man lined up originally. On back-up passes they cover the short one-quarter pass zones.

Linebackers—The linebackers line up on the inside eyes of the offensive tackles and play their regular positions. If the play comes toward a linebacker, he whips the blocker with a flipper and plays the ball-carrier. When the flow is away, he checks the counter play and then pursues the football. On pass plays he covers the short one-quarter pass zone.

Secondary—The defensive secondary plays its regular 3-deep coverage. On wide-running plays the halfback must come up to the outside and turn the play back in. The safety man comes up to the inside, playing inside-out, and the far halfback revolves and becomes the last safety man.

Figures 151—154 illustrate several of our defensive stunts from a 6-2 alignment which we have employed with success in the past.

In Figure 151 the linemen pinch, sealing-off the inside, and the linebackers cover outside.

In Figure 152 the guards loop to the outside over the offensive tackles, and the linebackers fill inside the offensive guard splits.

FIG. 151

FIG. 152

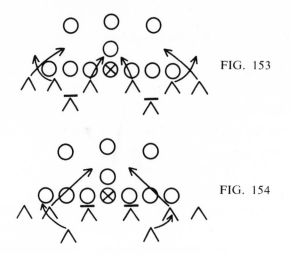

FIG. 153

FIG. 154

Figure 153 shows a simple X-pattern between the defensive ends and tackles.

Figure 154 illustrates the tackles pinching and the linebackers replacing them at the line of scrimmage over the offensive ends.

OUR DEFENSE AGAINST AN UNBALANCED LINE

Our adjustments against unbalanced lines are relatively simple. We merely move our defensive line over one whole man, and then revolve the secondary toward the weak side. (See Figure 155.)

When we do this, we carry out our same assignments, which have already been explained. The only difference is

FIG. 155

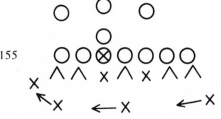

that our middle guard lines up on the offensive strong side guard, instead of on the center. If we are playing a 3-deep defense, we adjust with our linemen. Then we consider the strong guard as the middle of the offensive line (the center), and we play our regular defense.

ADJUSTMENTS AGAINST BACKS
AND ENDS FLANKED

When we have a defense called and the opposition lines up with a back or an end out, we can play it one of two ways. If it is a floater out or an end split, we adjust slightly with our secondary and drop the defensive end off the line a little. The remainder of the defensive linemen play the defense that has been called. If a flanker is put out to one side or the other, we revolve our 4-spoke secondary toward him and leave the linemen in their regular positions, or we shift our line toward the flanker one whole man.

In making our game plans, we always have a definite plan that our signal caller will use in the situations discussed above relating to our adjustments against backs and/or ends flanked out. For example, we may tell our signal caller to shift our defense *away* from ends out and floaters, but shift *toward* flankers and an unbalanced line. These calls will depend upon the information we secure from scouting our opponents.

OUR DEFENSES VERSUS
THE SINGLE WING OFFENSE

Defensing the Single Wing offense has always created problems for us because we feel we must meet strength with

strength, and then we get hurt to the weak side. Figures 156
and 157 illustrate two defenses that we have used successfully against the Single Wing offense.

Figure 156 is a defense which I feel is especially good
against the Single Wing offense. The duties of the defenders
are as follows:

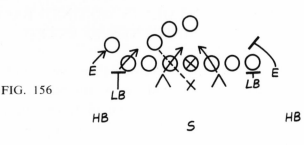

FIG. 156

Strong Side End—He lines up one to three yards outside
the wingback, "reading" him and the offensive end. If the
flow comes toward the strong side end he comes across
hard about three yards into the offensive backfield, and
turns everything in. When he makes contact with the outside blocker, the defensive end's shoulders must be parallel
to the line of scrimmage. If the flow goes away from him,
he drops back and pursues the ball carrier. On a straight
drop back pass, he covers the short one-quarter zone.

Strong Side Tackle—He lines up on the outside eye of
the offensive end. On the snap of the ball he charges through
the head of his man, penetrating the offense about one yard.
If the flow goes away, he trails the play. On a straight drop
back pass he rushes from the outside.

Strong Side Guard—He lines up on the outside eye of
the defensive guard. On the snap of the ball he tries to
penetrate through the head of the guard, sealing off the

middle. If the flow goes away, he pursues the ball. On a straight drop back pass he rushes from the inside.

Weak Side Guard—He has the same alignment and assignment as the strong side guard.

Weak Side Linebacker—He plays in front of the offensive weak side end and keeps him from getting out quickly on a pass play. If the flow comes toward him, the weak side linebacker whips the end and then "plays football." If the flow is away, he pursues the ball. On a straight drop back pass he covers the short flat one-quarter pass zone.

Weak Side End—He lines up about two yards outside of the offensive weak side end. If the flow comes toward him, he crosses the line playing his 8 technique. He cannot permit the play to get outside of his position. When he makes contact with the blocker, his shoulders must be parallel with the line of scrimmage. He trails the play if the flow goes away from him and rushes the passer on a drop back pass action.

Middle Linebacker—He lines up in front of the center, but his position varies some. At times he will be close to, and other times off, the offensive center's position. He keys the blocking back, who is the offensive quarterback, as the middle linebacker goes to the football. He drops back and covers the short one-quarter zone on drop back passes.

Strong Side Linebacker—He lines up behind the strong side tackle and reads the wingback, the end, and the quarterback. When the flow is toward him, he comes up and plays it tough. When the flow goes away from him he pursues the football. He covers a short one-quarter zone on a straight drop back pass.

3-Deep Secondary—They play their regular 3-deep coverage.

Figure 157 illustrates another of our 6-2 defensive alignments against the Single Wing offense. The individual assignments are the same as those just described, except that the
guards play more deliberately.

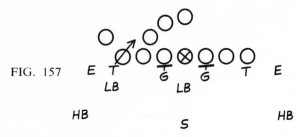

FIG. 157

We employ a number of defensive stunts when we play
against a Single Wing team. We have been quite successful
in the past with the stunts illustrated in Figures 158–161.
There are other stunts which may be used, of course, but
we have found these four stunts to be adequate.

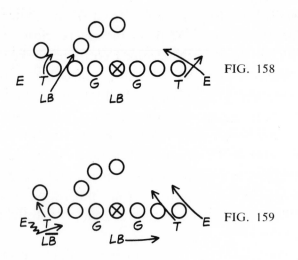

FIG. 158

FIG. 159

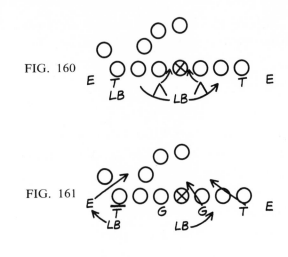

FIG. 160

FIG. 161

PASS DEFENSE*

Pass defense is so vital that one simple defensive mistake can cost the team a football game. In order to have a good team, the play in the defensive secondary must be sound.

The primary objective of pass defense is to keep the opponent from scoring. The second objective is to get the football. We stress these points all the time. On every play we want each player to try to get possession of the football for our team.

Pass defense consists of the following phases:

1. Rushing the passer.
2. Holding up receivers.
3. Covering the zones.

We have found it difficult to do a job of *all* three of these phases at the same time.

* From *Building A Championship Football Team* by Paul "Bear" Bryant (Englewood Cliffs, N. J.: Prentice-Hall, Inc., 1960), Chapter 5.

Rushing the Passer

Rushing the passer is a good element of surprise, especially with an 8- or 9-man line. Overloading one side of the line is a sound tactic, because then there are more men rushing than the offense has blocking and the quarterback must get rid of the ball quickly. If the quarterback has sufficient time to spot his receivers, and then is able to throw to one of them breaking into the open, it is difficult for the defense to cover the pass properly.

The men rushing the passer must have their hands up high, forcing the passer to release the ball higher than he does normally. Such tactics will keep the passer from throwing the fast, straight, bullet-like pass, which is the hardest for the defenders to break up. Secondly, the rushers with their hands high cause the pass to remain in the air longer because of its upward trajectory as it is released. Consequently, the defensive secondary has time to release from their areas and sprint to the spot where the ball is descending.

The man who has the outside rush, and whose responsibility it is to contain, must get his hands high. He should *not* leap off the ground in an effort to tackle the passer, as he must be in a position to contain him in the event the passer tries to get out of the pocket.

When we are rushing the passer, we want our players to know that they *must not* permit the passer to throw the football. In a definite passing situation when we decide to overload a zone and rush more men than the opposition has blockers, we realize that we are sacrificing coverage in our secondary. Therefore, we must put on a strong rush and we cannot permit the ball to be thrown.

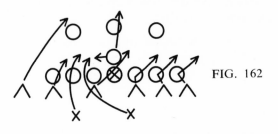

FIG. 162

Figure 162 illustrates an overload on the right side of the offensive line. Assuming it is a passing situation when we overload, if the opposition does throw a drop back pass we are in good position because we have more rushers than they have blockers. If the opposition runs to their right, which would be to our left, we are still sound defensively because they are running into our strength. In other words, we are 66⅔ per cent correct before the play even starts. If the opposition goes to their left (our right), we are not strong, but because our right side is hitting and sliding to the outside, as is shown in Figure 162, we will not be hurt.

There are many ways of rushing a passer, but we do not expect to do a really good job of rushing unless we outnumber the blockers. Then, when we have a pass rush called, our boys know they must not permit the passer to throw the ball.

Holding Up Receivers

We work on detaining the receivers at the line of scrimmage, but we probably do not devote enough time to this phase of pass defense. The purpose of this defensive tactic is to give the linebackers time to get to their defensive areas before the receivers get to them. It also gives the defensive halfbacks time to get their width and depth and get set up in their respective pass coverage zones. We hold up receivers in several different ways, as is illustrated in Figures 163-165.

Figure 163 illustrates the tackle playing head up on the offensive end in order to detain him.

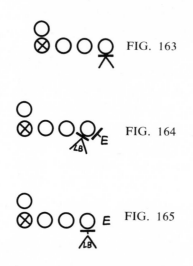

FIG. 163

FIG. 164

FIG. 165

Figure 164 illustrates the defensive end and linebacker pinching off the offensive end, making it difficult for him to release for a pass.

Figure 165 illustrates a third method of holding up an eligible receiver. The linebacker lines up in front of the offensive end so he can "whack" him as he releases from the line of scrimmage.

Covering the Areas

We cover zones on pass defense and not the eligible receivers. We want our players to be in the middle of their zones in a good football position. As soon as the ball leaves

the passer's hand, we want our boys to forget about everything else *except intercepting the pass*. They should play
through the receiver *for* the ball and should never go around
the receiver, unless it is a short pass. Also, they should go
for the ball at the highest point they can reach. Our logic
is that if a defender is waiting for the ball to come down
so he can handle it at his chest or waist, the intended
receiver has time to come in front of our defender and
catch the pass for completion. Whereas, if our defender
will go back when the ball is thrown, plant, and come
toward the opponent's goal line intercepting the ball with
arms and fingers extended upward, the intended receiver
can't possibly take the ball away from him.

CONCLUSION

There are many defenses that are good against various
offensive formations. The important point is to have a defense that you and your players believe in, and which is
sound in all respects. Each player must take pride in himself
and his defensive ability. He must personally feel that he
is not going to permit the opposition to score. He must
accept this as a personal challenge to himself. He must
eliminate the long run and/or the long pass for the "easy"
touchdown, and he must pursue relentlessly and tackle
viciously in order to have a sound defense.

CHAPTER TWELVE

Scouting Opponents

Darrell Royal
University of Texas

DARRELL ROYAL, head coach at the University of Texas since 1957, has engineered one of the most remarkable recovery programs in collegiate football. Taking a team that had finished in the Southwest Conference cellar the year before with a 1-9 overall record, Royal has led Texas to an impressive 39-13-2 five-year record, including action in four major bowl games.

The 1961 Longhorns, compiling a 9-1 record, were praised by Royal as the best team he had ever coached. They were among the nation's offensive leaders all season as they tied for the conference title and won the 1962 Cotton Bowl with a stunning 12-7 win over Mississippi. Following the 1961 season, Royal was named Coach of the Year by the Football Writers Association of America.

During his collegiate days at the University of Oklahoma, Royal was known for his versatility on the gridiron. He was an outstanding halfback, punter, quarterback, and defensive player. As a senior in 1949, Royal won consensus all-American honors when he quarterbacked one of Oklahoma's finest teams.

Before joining the Texas staff, Royal coached at North Carolina State, Tulsa, Mississippi State, and the University of Washington.

Scouting Opponents

Scouting has become a very important part of football in recent years. To prepare his team adequately, the coach must know as much as he can, in advance, about opponents—about the capabilities of their personnel, the formations they use, the plays they run, the tendencies of their offense, the defenses they employ, and their strengths and weaknesses. The more a coach and his players know about a team that they are going to play, the better chance they will have of defeating them.

Requirements of the Scout

The football scout must first have a sound knowledge of the game of football. In an ideal situation, the scout will be as well-versed in the game as the head coach.

The scout must also be an alert person who has trained himself to see as many things as possible in a football game. When an untrained person watches a left halfback run off-tackle, that is probably *all* he sees. But an experienced football scout watching the same play sees how the offense is set up, how the blocking develops, and the exact path of the ball-carrier.

The Use of Films in Scouting

Scouting has become a much more exacting science in recent years because of the more concentrated study of motion picture films. Details that would be missed while watching the actual game are easy to see when the film of each play can be run back and forth as many times as the coach feels is necessary.

During the summer our scouts get films of the last four games that each team we are scouting played the previous season. The scouts study these films of the opposing teams to get a run-down on their personnel and to see if their attack has varied any since our last game with them. We study the actions of any players that are returning, the changes in the team's offensive attack and in its defenses, and the defensive adjustments to different formations.

After a scout has looked at films of a team every day for a month during the summer, he begins to feel that he knows the opposing team pretty well. In fact, he knows almost as much about the team he is scouting as he does about his own team.

Our staff at the University of Texas is divided into offensive and defensive groups. The coaches that are concerned with defense spend a week in the summer on each opposing team, studying their offense. The offensive coaches spend the same time studying the opponents' defenses. During these sessions the "Film Take Off Charts" are prepared. (See Figures 166 and 167.)

Some of the information that we get on teams can only be obtained through films. For example, a team's defensive keys cannot be scouted without films. Learning all of a team's keys while watching a game would require the use of several scouts, each one watching one individual player throughout the game. Yet, defensive keys are not too difficult to pick out from a film.

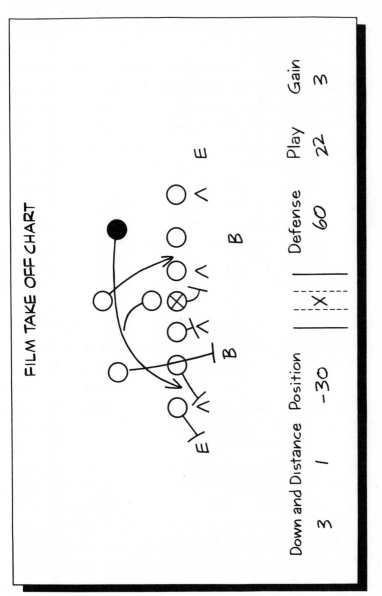

FIG. 166

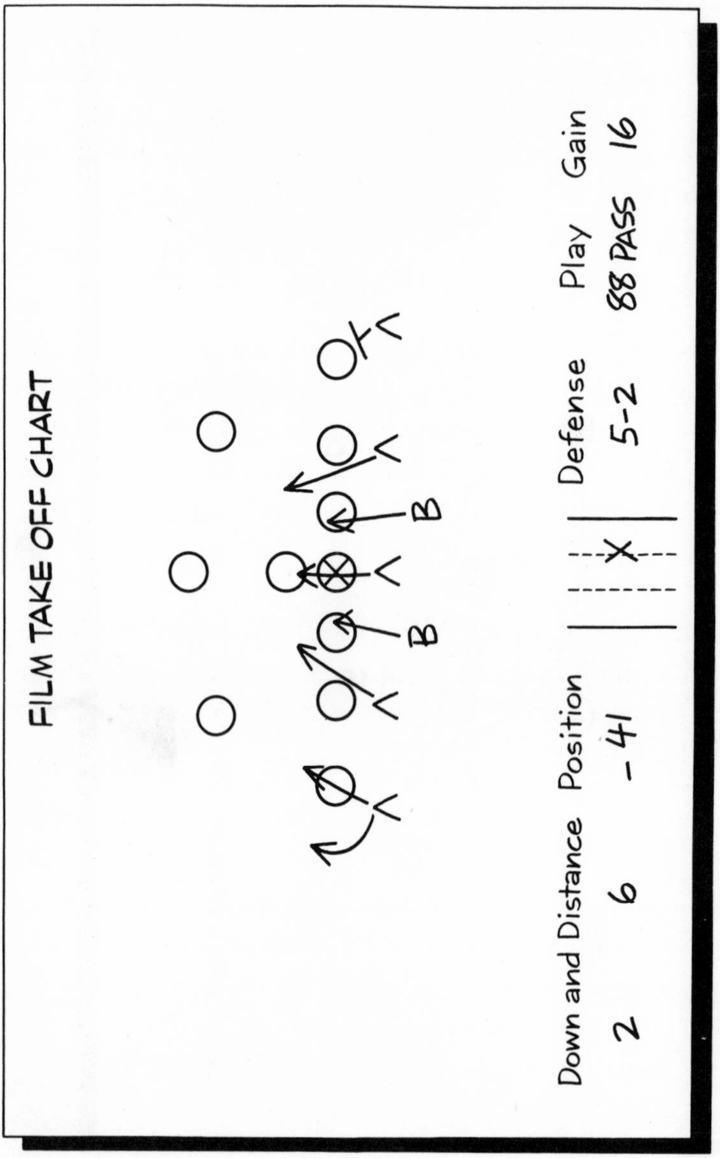

FIG. 167

On the other hand, there are certain game situations that spread players out beyond the limits of the movie frame, making it impossible to scout that particular play adequately from a film. Kick off and punt returns, pass patterns, some defensive backfield positions, and certain spread formations are difficult or impossible to scout adequately through films.

Summer Preparations for Scouting

During the summer the groundwork is laid for the scouting that will be done in the fall. Besides the hours spent studying films of the coming season's opponents, plans are made for scouting them in person.

We feel that we should plan to scout each team at least twice during the season if possible. The more a scout sees a team, the more he will know about them.

And we try to see each team against teams that are similar to ours in ability. If our scouts see a team playing an inferior opponent, they might not even see the same players that will be playing against us.

Information from Newspapers

Coaches are able to get some information on opposing teams from newspaper articles. Each scout should subscribe to all newspapers from cities where the teams he is to scout are located. The coach should clip out anything in the papers about the teams he is to scout and put the information in his file.

Maurice Doke, all-American guard at Texas.

Scouting the Game

Our scouts arrive at the stadium at least an hour before game time and go to their seats in the pressbox or in the stands.

While the team is warming up, we find out who their punters are, how long it takes them to get their kicks away, how far they kick the ball, how high they kick it, and how deep they stand in the backfield.

We use a stop watch on the centers and kickers to see if we should plan to return their punts or concentrate on trying to block them. If the kicker is getting the ball away in a hurry, we may as well drop back and return the kick. But if he is not getting the ball off quickly, we will try to block it.

We also see who the kick off men are and make a note of how high and how far they kick the ball.

It is difficult to tell much about passers by watching them during the warmup, since some passers react differently under pressure from rushers than they do when warming up. The scout may learn something of the distances they throw and the patterns they like, but to really know the passers well the scout must see them throw during the game.

In the actual observing and recording of the game, we use the "Offensive Take Off Chart" to keep a running account of every offensive play. (See Figure 168.) On it we record the down, distance, position on the field in relation to the goal lines and hash marks, the formation, the defense used against it, the play, and the gain or loss on the play.

To record the team's defenses we use the "Defensive Take Off Chart." (See Figure 169.) On it we record the team's

OFFENSIVE TAKE OFF CHART

Number of Play	Down	Distance	Position	Hash	Formation	Defense	Play	Gain
1	1	10	-25	R	CR	60	18 Sweep	+12
2	1	10	-37	R	CR	"	32	+9
3	2	1	-46	R	CR Fly	"	19 Sweep	+5
4	1	10	+49	L	CL Fly	"	19 Reverse	+16
5	1	10	+33	L	CL Fly	"	32	+3
6	2	7	+30	L	CL Fly	"	18 Sweep	+6
7	3	1	+24	R	CR Fly	"	25	+1
8	1	10	+23	M	CR	"	52	—
9	2	10	+23	M	CL	"	19 Sweep	+5
10	3	5	+18	L	CRW	"	88 Pass	TD

FIG. 168

DEFENSIVE TAKE OFF CHART

2nd QUARTER

DOWN	DIST.	POS.	HASH	DEFENSE	PLAY	GAIN	COMMENTS AND DEFENSIVE ALIGNMENT
1	10	-30	L	60	24	3	
2	7	-33	M	5-4	54	9	
1	10	-42	M	60	26	1	
2	9	-43	L	5-4	55	4	
3	5	-47	R	5-4	24P	-	
4	5	-47	R		Punt		
1	10	-22	M	60	52	2	
2	8	-24	M	5-4	52P	1	
3	8	-24	M	5-4	52P	19	
1	10	-43	R	60	27	2	
2	8	-45	M	5-4	52P	1	
3	8	-45	M	5-4	98P	4	
4	4	-49	M		Punt		

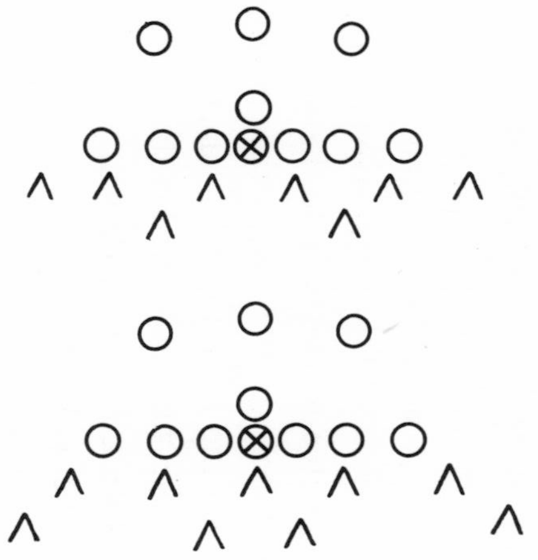

FIG. 169

basic defenses, as well as the adjustments they make to flankers, wingbacks, and split ends. We also record the down, distance, position on the field, hash mark, play, gain or loss, and any comments on the defenses used.

When two scouts work a game together, one describes the play while the other writes down the information. When only one scout is watching a game, he takes note of the offensive formation and the defensive alignment and watches the play. As the team goes back to the huddle, he records the name or number of the play, the down, the distance, the position on the field and hash mark, the formation, the defense, and the gain or loss. To the beginning scout this might seem like a lot of writing in a very short time, but with practice he will soon learn to get it all down with time to spare.

Besides the "Offensive and Defensive Take Off Charts," scouts should always have a large pad of paper for recording pass patterns, kickoff and punt returns, and anything of significance about personnel.

The scout can best visualize an entire offensive play by focusing his attention on the quarterback and guards. If one guard pulls and traps as the fullback goes up the middle, the scout knows that the play is a fullback trap. If, however, he had followed the ball and had seen the fullback go up the middle, the scout would not have known whether it was a trap play or not.

Also, a scout can tell immediately if it is a pass play by watching the guards. If the guards "set" to protect the passer, the scout should start looking for the ends and halfbacks so that he can get the pass pattern.

Every team has a few favorite plays. We take particular note of plays that the team relies on when they face tough situations. Any play might be called in first-and-ten or third-and-one situations, but the quarterback is going to call on his top personnel and his two or three best plays when the down is third-and-five or when they are within the ten-yard line trying to push over for a score. These are the plays that we are going to have to stop.

In scouting defenses, we watch the entire team rather than individual players. We see what defenses are used on long yardage, medium yardage, and short yardage. We also want to know the defensive alignments when they are on their end of the field and when they are on ours, and what adjustments they make to various formations. In short, we want to know what our offense can expect to be faced with in any given situation when we play this team later in the season.

Charting the Team

When our scouts return home after a game, they begin making out the various charts from the "Offensive and Defensive Take Off Charts" that they completed at the game.

On the "Hash Mark Tendency Chart," the scouts record the plays the team used and at which holes these plays were run in relation to the hash marks. (See Figure 170.)

Next they make out the "Formation Play Graph." (See Figure 171.) On this chart they record the plays run at the various holes from the different formations.

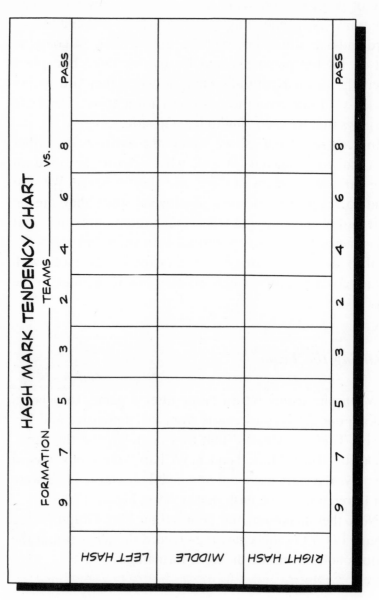

FIG. 170

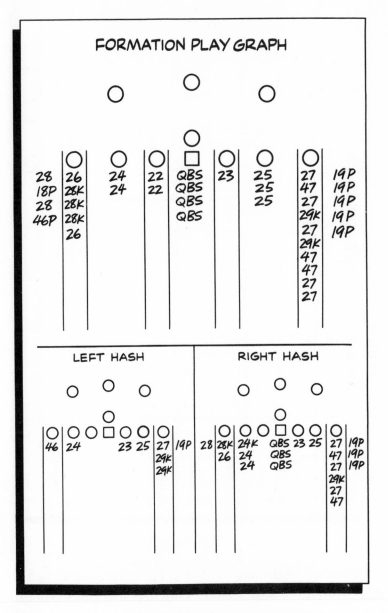

FIG. 171

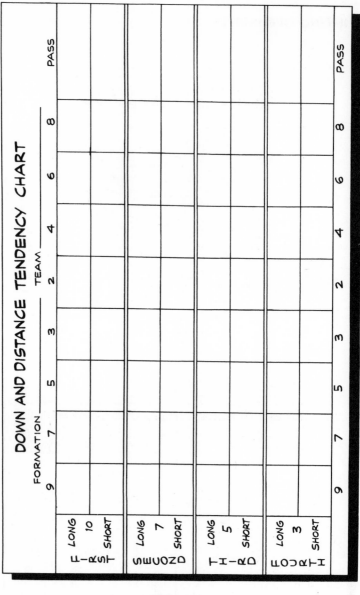

FIG. 172

Then the "Down and Distance Tendency Chart" is filled out. (See Figure 172.) Every play that was run during the game is recorded on this chart, under the hole and across from the down and distance column.

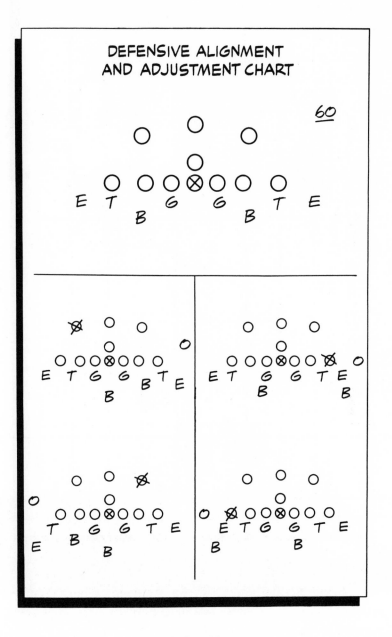

FIG. 173

James Saxton, all-American halfback at Texas.

The one defensive chart that our scouts fill out is the "Defensive Alignment and Adjustment Chart." (See Figure 173.) This chart tells us the team's defenses and the adjustments that they make when the offensive formation has flanked halfbacks or split ends.

The "Offensive and Defensive Film Take Off Charts," shown on pages 238 and 239, show us in great detail how the team's plays are run. These charts are filled out by our scouts during the previous summer from films of last year's games. They tell us the exact plays the team is running, complete with every blocking assignment, and the exact defenses they use.

The "Hash Mark Tendency Chart" and the "Down and Distance Tendency Chart" can tell the coach a great deal about a team's offense. Quarterbacks have a tendency to do certain things in certain situations, often subconsciously, and it is difficult for them to change. From the tendency charts, we are able to tell what the quarterback is likely to call in those situations, and we prepare our defenses accordingly.

Game Strategy Based on Scouting

Much of our game strategy is based on the opposing team's tendencies—both offensively and defensively. In most situations we will have a good idea what plays will be run against us and what defenses will be used to try to stop our attack.

If our scouting report shows an apparent weakness in the opposing team's defenses, we will plan to direct our attack at it. And, conversely, if they have a strong point, we try to stay away from it. When playing a team that has an outstanding tackle, for example, we would try to run away from him as much as possible.

We may add one or two new plays to our offense from week to week, but we always stay with the basic offense that we have used all season. Rather than change our style of attack for a new team, we simply concentrate on a particular phase of it.

The same is true of our defense. Rather than change the defenses that we have been using all season, we try to strengthen them in the areas where the opponent is strong.

Occasionally we will put in a new play to take advantage of a team's defensive keys. For example, a team using a 5-4 defense might have each cornerback and defensive half-back keying the halfback on his side. (See Figure 174.)

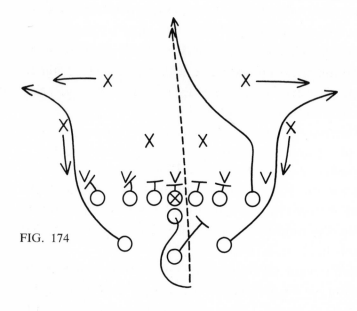

FIG. 174

When the offensive halfback moves forward, the cornerback on his side moves toward the line of scrimmage and the defensive halfback moves to the outside.

If we knew in advance that a team was doing this, we would send both halfbacks into the flat, pulling the defensive halfbacks with them, and send one of our ends down the middle for the pass.

Situations like this do not often present themselves, but when they do, an alert coach can take advantage of them.

Presenting the Scouting Report to the Squad

Before practice on Monday, we have a short general meeting of the squad and coaching staff to discuss the week's opponent.

On Tuesday and Wednesday, I meet with our quarterbacks at lunch and again before practice to discuss our opponent's defenses and defensive tendencies. At these same times, the defensive coach meets with our defensive signal-callers to go over our opponent's offense, their offensive tendencies, and their favorite plays.

On Thursday afternoon, we show the entire squad one quarter of a game that the opponent has played recently.

In practice during the week, we go over the material covered on the "Hash Mark Tendency Chart" and the "Formation Play Graph." The squad is told what to expect in certain situations—what plays will probably be called and who is likely to be the ball-carrier.

We don't want to burden our players with too much information, so we give them only four or five of the opponent's plays to learn. These plays are diagrammed on the board and the third team runs them against the varsity during the week.

We also pass out a scouting report to each squad member. (See Figures 175-182.) Included in this report are the name, number, age, and size of each player, where he plays on offense and defense, and the number of years he has played. (Much of this information can be taken from the game program when the team is scouted.)

If possible, a rundown on some of the players' capabilities should be included in the report. If the opposition has an outstanding back or lineman, we want our players to know it. And if a particular player has a tendency to loaf, we want them to know that, too.

The rest of the report includes a breakdown of the plays that the team has run during the past two games and the defenses that they used. This might seem like a lot of information, but when it is put into graph form, it gives the squad an excellent over-all picture of what to expect from the opponent.

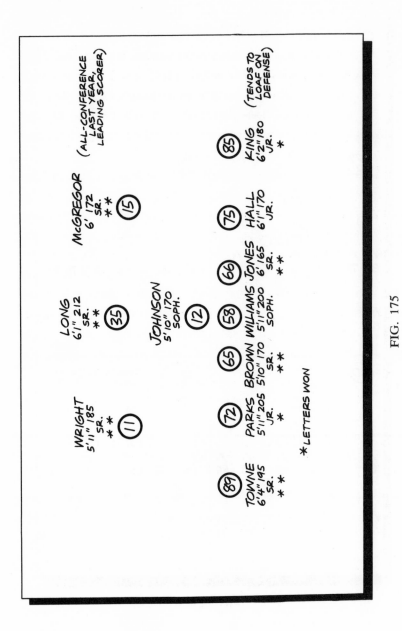

FIG. 175

STATE DEFENSE

State will play a 60 defense most of the time. They will also play a 61-62 to our wing or to the wide side.

State will definitely overshift over our tackles. #65 will play on both sides of the middle guard to form their overshift. They are not a penetrating defense nor do they stunt very much.

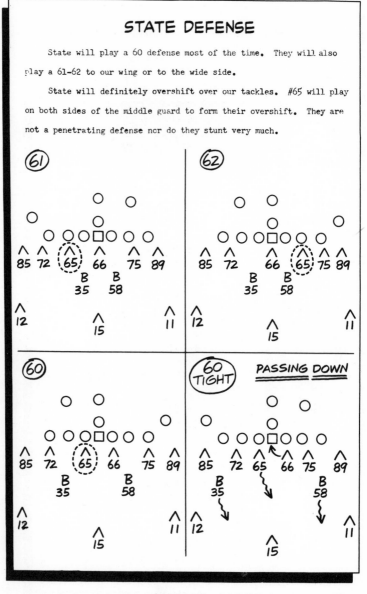

FIG. 176

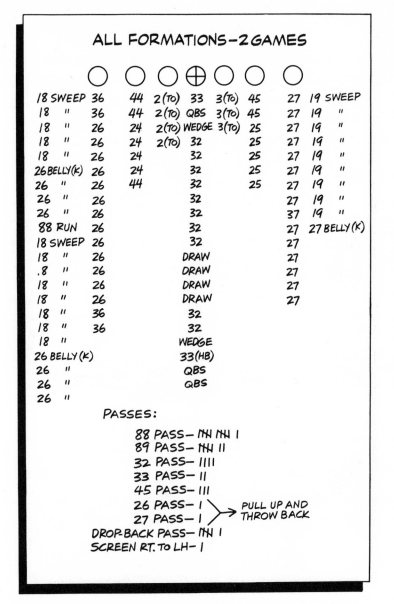

FIG. 177

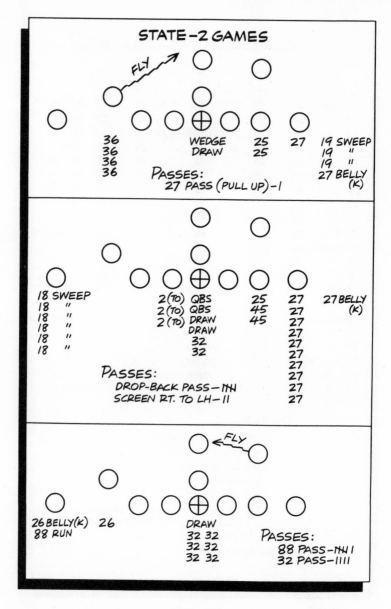

FIG. 178

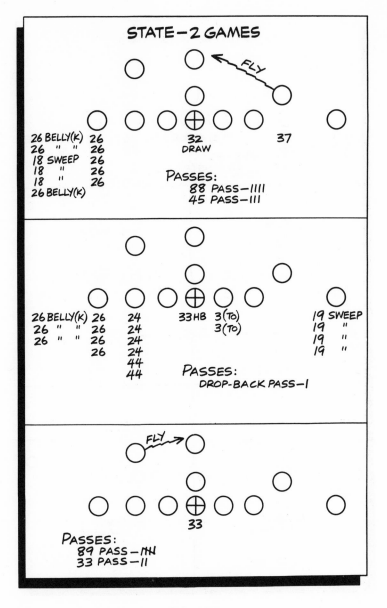

FIG. 179

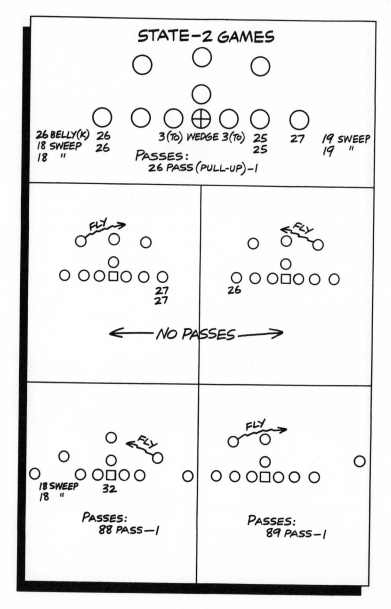

FIG. 180

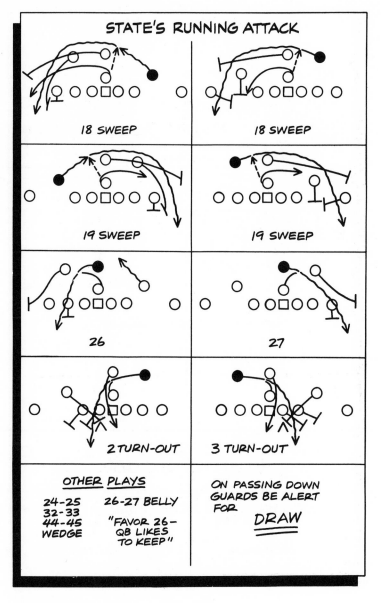

FIG. 181

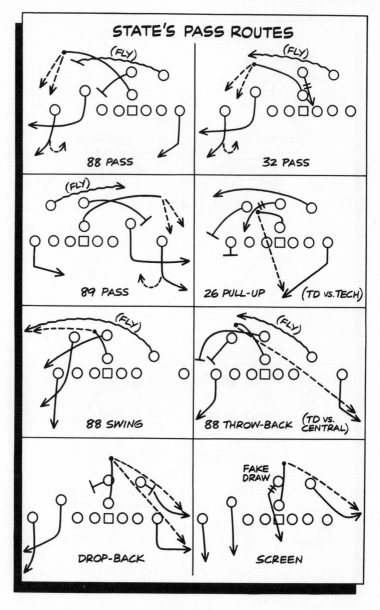

FIG. 182

Index